How shall we sing
the LORD's song in a strange land?
Psalm 137:4, KJV

The Bible Speaks Today

Series Editors: J. A. Motyer (OT)
 John R. W. Stott (NT)

Songs from a Strange Land

Psalms 42—51

John Goldingay

InterVarsity Press
Downers Grove
Illinois 60515

© *John Goldingay, 1978*
First American printing, July 1978, by
InterVarsity Press, with permission from
Universities and Colleges Christian Fellowship,
Leicester, England.

InterVarsity Press is the book-publishing
division of Inter-Varsity Christian Fellowship,
a student movement active on campus
at hundreds of universities, colleges and
schools of nursing. For information
about local and regional activities, write
IVCF, 233 Langdon St., Madison, WI 53703.

Distributed in Canada through Inter-Varsity
Press, 1875 Leslie St., Unit 10,
Don Mills, Ontario M3B 2M5, Canada.

ISBN 0-87784-799-1
Library of Congress
Catalog Card Number: 78-2078

Printed in the United States of America

General Preface

The Bible speaks today describes a projected series of both Old and New Testament expositions, which are characterized by a threefold ideal: to expound the biblical text with accuracy, to relate it to contemporary life, and to be readable.

These books are, therefore, not 'commentaries', for the commentary seeks rather to elucidate the text than to apply it, and tends to be a work rather of reference than of literature. Nor, on the other hand, do they contain the kind of 'sermons' which attempt to be contemporary and readable, without taking Scripture seriously enough.

The contributors to this series will all be united in their convictions that God still speaks through what he has spoken, and that nothing is more necessary for the life, growth and health of churches or of Christians than that they should hear and heed what the Spirit is saying to them through his ancient—yet ever modern—Word.

J. A. MOTYER
J. R. W. STOTT
Series Editors

Contents

Author's Preface

MY feelings as I have been completing these expositions may be expressed in words borrowed from two great expositors.

'They have made a Rule in the Council of Trent, that no Scripture shall be expounded, but according to the unanime consent of the Fathers: But in this Book of the Psalms, it would trouble them to give many examples of that Rule, that is, of an unanime consent of the Fathers, in the interpretation thereof' (Donne, p. 45).

The reader who compares several standard translations of the Bible will find that they, too, vary considerably in their rendering of the Psalms. Although sometimes this difference is only a matter of style, often it does involve disagreement as to what the Hebrew words mean or as to what the writers' words actually were. Not that we are uncertain as to the general significance of the Psalms; but there is debate over very many points of detail. I have had to come to my own conclusions on these points, and they are embodied in the translation which accompanies the exposition. But in an expository commentary of this kind it is not possible to include the justification of all the debated points, for which I can only refer the reader to the commentaries and other works listed under 'Chief Abbreviations' and referred to in the footnotes.[1]

[1] There is one way in which I am aware that my translation differs from RSV, NEB, JB, *etc.* In most psalms there are several points at which these translations assume that what the psalmist wrote has been changed by the time MT was produced, and they therefore emend the text of the Hebrew before trans-

I hope, at any rate,

'That there should not need another Comment upon my comment, that when I pretend to interpret the Psalme, they that heare me, should not need another to interpret me: which is frequent infirmity amongst Expositors of Scriptures' (Donne, pp. 46–47, himself quoting from Jerome).

As far as the task of exegesis is concerned, however, and at least as much with the challenge of exposition,

'I cannot promise that I shall lecture satisfactorily, for I admit that I have not fully grasped the Spirit who speaks there. Still it gives us an opportunity and a basis for thought and study, so that I can become a student with you and await the Spirit. Whatever He gives, we shall receive with thanks' (Luther, p. 303).

Whatever the inadequacies of my attempts to open the curtains and let the light shine out of God's Word, it will be enough if they encourage the reader himself to investigate (and to allow himself to be investigated by) that Word, for deep treasures are there. Indeed,

'David . . . remains a pupil with us; for all men, be they ever so illumined by the Holy Spirit, still remain pupils of the Word. They remain under and near the Word, and they experience that they can hardly draw out a drop from the vast ocean of the Holy Spirit' (Luther, p. 305).

My involvement with these psalms goes back to the time some years ago when I had to study them as a set text, but I first came to expound some of them in Bible Readings in St John's College chapel in 1973. I am grateful to members of St John's also for the discussions on the psalms that we have had together in seminars,

---

lating it. They usually indicate in the margin that they have done this. As I have examined the various emendations accepted by these translations (and others proposed by scholars) I find myself only very rarely convinced that the emendation is more likely than the received Hebrew text: it is often possible and plausible, but not, I find, compelling. In this sense my translation is rather conservative compared with the standard modern ones. 42:5; 44:4; 49:14 and 51:8 provide examples.

and for the freedom which the college gave me to work at this manuscript during a sabbatical term in 1975.

It is appropriate for me to express my appreciation in certain other directions, and I do so gladly: to Alec Motyer, who has not only offered an editor's clear but tactful guidance, but also bears a fair amount of the responsibility both for my interest in the Old Testament, and for my approach to exposition; to Miss Dorothy Gould, who read my typescript with care and enabled me to correct many slips; and to my wife Ann. At critical moments, it is through the Psalms that the Lord has spoken to us together.

'Whom have I in heaven but thee?
And there is nothing upon earth that I desire besides thee.'
73:25, RSV   21 April 1966

'When the Lord turned again the captivity of Sion: then were we like unto them that dream.'

126:1, PBV   6 May 1975

St John's College,   JOHN GOLDINGAY
Nottingham

Chief Abbreviations

As well as providing a key to the abbreviations by which I have referred to general works, the list below includes the works on the Psalms to which I am conscious of being indebted. These are referred to by the author's name (the reference, in the case of commentaries, being to the discussion of the passage in question), though I have not tried systematically to attribute every idea.

Anderson	A. A. Anderson, *The Book of Psalms*, vol. 1 (*New Century Bible*, Oliphants, 1972).
AV	Authorized (King James') Version of the Bible, 1604–11.
BDB	F. Brown, S. R. Driver and C. A. Briggs, *A Hebrew and English Lexicon of the Old Testament* (OUP, reprinted 1962).
BHS	*Biblia Hebraica Stuttgartensia: Liber Psalmorum*, ed. H. Bardtke (Württembergische Bibelanstalt, 1969).
Birkeland	H. Birkeland, *The Evildoers in the Book of Psalms* (Almqvist & Wiksells, 1955).
Briggs	C. A. and E. G. Briggs, *A Critical and Exegetical Commentary on the Book of Psalms* (*International Critical Commentary*, T. & T. Clark, 1907).
Brockington	L. H. Brockington, *The Hebrew Text of the Old Testament: The Readings Adopted by the Translators of the New English Bible* (OUP and CUP, 1973).

Calvin   J. Calvin, *Commentary on the Book of Psalms*, vol. II (ET, Eerdmans, reprinted 1949).

Dahood   M. J. Dahood, *Psalms* (*The Anchor Bible*, Doubleday, 1965–70).

Dalglish   E. R. Dalglish, *Psalm Fifty-One* (Brill, 1962).

Delitzsch   F. Delitzsch, *Biblical Commentary on the Psalms* (ET, *Foreign Biblical Library*, Hodder & Stoughton, ²1902).

Donne   *John Donne's Sermons on the Psalms and Gospels*, ed. E. M. Simpson (University of California Press, 1963).

Eaton   J. H. Eaton, *Psalms: Introduction and Commentary* (*Torch Bible Commentaries*, SCM Press, 1967).

Eichrodt   W. Eichrodt, *Theology of the Old Testament* (ET, *Old Testament Library*, SCM Press, 1961–67).

ET   English translation.

EVV   English versions.

Gelineau   *The Psalms: A New Translation from the Hebrew Arranged for Singing to the Psalmody of Joseph Gelineau* (Collins Fontana Books, 1966).

GK   *Gesenius' Hebrew Grammar as edited and enlarged by the late E. Kautzsch* (ET, Clarendon Press,² reprinted 1966).

Gunkel   H. Gunkel, *Die Psalmen* (Vandenhoeck und Ruprecht, ⁵1968).

Jastrow   M. Jastrow, *A Dictionary of the Targumim, the Talmud Babli and Yerushalmi, and the Midrashic Literature* (Verlag Choreb, 1926).

JB   *The Jerusalem Bible* (Darton, Longman & Todd, 1966).

KB   L. Koehler and W. Baumgartner, *Lexicon in Veteris Testamenti Libros* (Brill, 1953).

Kidner   Derek Kidner, *Psalms* (*Tyndale Old Testament Commentaries*, IVP, 1973–75).

Knight   G. A. F. Knight, *A Christian Theology of the Old Testament* (SCM Press, 1959, ²1964).

Kraus   H.-J. Kraus, *Psalmen*, I. Teilband (*Biblischer Kommentar Altes Testament*, Neukirchener Verlag, ³1966).

Luther	*Luther's Works*, vol. 12: *Selected Psalms* I, ed. J. Pelikan (ET, Concordia Publishing House, 1955).
LXX	The Septuagint (pre-Christian Greek translation of the Old Testament).
mg.	margin.
Mowinckel	S. Mowinckel, *The Psalms in Israel's Worship* (ET, Blackwell, 1967).
MS(S)	manuscript(s).
MT	Massoretic Text (the mainstream Hebrew text, edited by the Massoretes, which is the point of departure for EVV; note that its versification sometimes differs from that of EVV, which is used in this volume).
NEB	*The New English Bible: The Old Testament* (OUP and CUP, 1970).
PBV	'Prayer Book Version' of the Psalms, from the Great Bible (1539).
Pedersen	J. Pedersen, *Israel I–II* (OUP, 1926).
van der Ploeg	J. van der Ploeg, 'Notes sur le Psaume XLIX', in *Oudtestamentische Studiën* 13 (1963): *Studies on Psalms*, pp. 137–172.
Prothero	R. E. Prothero, *The Psalms in Human Life* (J. Murray, reprinted 1905).
von Rad	G. von Rad, *Old Testament Theology* (ET, Oliver & Boyd, reprinted 1967).
RSV	Revised Standard Version of the Bible, 1946–52.
Snaith	N. H. Snaith, *Hymns of the Temple* (SCM Press, 1951).
TDNT	G. Kittel and G. Friedrich (ed.), *Theological Dictionary of the New Testament* (ET, Eerdmans, 1964–74).
TEV	*Good News Bible: Today's English Version* (The Bible Societies, Collins Fontana, 1976).
de Vaux	R. de Vaux, *Ancient Israel: Its Life and Institutions* (ET, Darton, Longman & Todd, 1961).
Weiser	A. Weiser, *The Psalms: A Commentary* (ET, *Old Testament Library*, SCM Press, 1962).

Westermann   C. Westermann, *The Praise of God in the Psalms* (ET, Epworth Press, 1966).

Winton Thomas   D. Winton Thomas, *The Text of the Revised Psalter* (SPCK, 1963).

Introduction

THE great value of the Psalms is that 'most of Scripture speaks to us, while the Psalms speak *for* us'. That remark attributed to Athanasius[1] captures something of the importance of the Psalter in the Bible. Here are scores of examples of the things we can say to God. The Psalms do, of course, give expression to many points of theology. Their worship often means to address itself horizontally as well as vertically: they are concerned to honour God by declaring his praise before men. They sometimes explicitly speak God-to-man or man-to-man; but nevertheless their fundamental aim is to speak on man's behalf to God. They appear in Scripture as models of the prayer and protest, the thanksgiving and praise, which are acceptable to Yahweh the God of Israel, who is also the God and Father of our Lord Jesus Christ.

Different ways of speaking to God

Parents customarily put in a great deal of effort to get their children into the habit of saying 'please' and 'thank you', and there remains something fundamental about these two types of human speech. They appear also in men's speech with God, as we have already hinted, in the form of prayer and praise, or (to use terms that correspond more with the Psalms) lament and testimony.

The psalms of lament are urgent prayers uttered in situations of need, perhaps the military defeat and humiliation of the nation

[1] *Cf.* B. W. Anderson, *Out of the Depths* (Westminster Press, 1973), p. x.

(*e.g.* Ps. 44), perhaps the affliction, illness or persecution of the individual (*e.g.* Pss. 42–43). These laments have certain regular features. They are dominated by a detailed description of the psalmist's need (hence the title 'lament'—the prayers in the book of Lamentations are examples of these psalms of lament). The actual request is usually expressed only in general terms ('turn and save us': *cf.* 44:23–26), and the psalmist looks forward to returning to thank God when he has been delivered (51:13–15) —indeed he often (perhaps in response to a word of assurance from the Lord's representative) begins praising God even now for the deliverance he is confident of (*cf.* 42:5, 11; 43:5, NEB).

The psalms of praise and thanksgiving are first the vehicles whereby God's people give public testimony to the fact that God has answered their prayers. Sometimes the psalmists recall the actual affliction in which they prayed and from which God rescued them. There is thus a close link between lament and testimony, or prayer and praise. Prayer looks forward to praise, praise looks back to the incident about which prayer had to be made. It is not only God's specific recent deeds that he is praised for, however. In praise God's people rejoice in and testify to the fundamental deeds whereby he made them his people—to his acts of redemption. They praise him for his creation, for his revelation, for his presence in his city and in his temple with his people. They praise him for who he is: for after all, human speech does not begin with 'please' and 'thank you' but with a simpler recognition of and response to the person ('Daddy', 'Mummy'). Beyond 'please' and 'thank you' this is where it ends, too, with 'I love you' or 'You are smashing' or a wordless gaze. So it is with God: he is named and acknowledged for himself. (For some of these aspects of praise, see Pss. 46–48.)

Not all the psalms fit these two categories of lament and testimony: we shall be looking at three psalms which are not addressed Godward at all, but manward (45, a wedding psalm; 49, a wisdom psalm; 50, a psalm of judgment). But an impressive number do give expression to the prayer, thanksgiving or worship of community or individual, and comparing like with like helps both to see the general drift of a particular genre and also helps to see what is distinctive in an individual example.

The background of the Psalms

The Psalter is Israel's hymnbook. When we look at our hymns, we can consider their background in at least two ways. We may see them as arising out of specific incidents in the lives of their writers. Well-known stories are attached to hymns such as 'Just as I am' (which arose out of a spiritual crisis in Charlotte Elliott's life) and 'God moves in a mysterious way' (written after the melancholic Cowper failed in an attempt to commit suicide). But these circumstances of their origin do not influence what the hymns mean in Christian worship. Usually, indeed, a congregation will not be aware of such background information as the stories referred to above. The hymns gain their meaning from their ability to express what the congregation itself wants to say to God. The background of the hymns is not the historical circumstances of their origin but their use in the life of the church.

The same two approaches may be taken to the Psalms. We may be able to identify the historical origin of some: the psalms in the book of Lamentations, for instance, clearly belong to the exile. The headings of some psalms may indicate their authorship and thus their background, though most often these are liturgical notes of some kind. The content of other psalms (*e.g.* Ps. 48) suggests some incident in the history of the Israelite nation. Others, however (*e.g.* Pss. 42–43), offer us no such clue. Such psalms arose out of some real personal situation, but we do not know what it was. Yet somehow this does not greatly affect the meaningfulness of the psalms to us. What matters is not exactly what circumstances surrounded their origin, but what they meant to Israel.

This leads us into looking at the psalms' other background, in the life of the Israelite people. This will be primarily their life of worship, as is the case with our hymnbook. Like the church's year, Israel's religious year included certain great festivals. The laws make special mention of Passover and Unleavened Bread in the spring, Pentecost in high summer, and the Day of Atonement and Tabernacles in the autumn (when the rains were due and thus the agricultural year began). Many of our hymns connect with such festivals as Easter and Christmas, and it is likely that many of the psalms similarly connected with Israel's festivals. Themes which might be expected to feature at such festivals appear in some psalms, and thus various connections with festivals have been suggested. Psalm 50, for instance, describes the declaring of God's judgment, on the basis of the covenant made with him at Mount Sinai and embodied in his commandments, and we are reminded of the prescription in Deuteronomy for the reading of the law at the feast of Tabernacles, to remind Israel of her covenant obligations (Dt. 31:10–13). Psalm 47, like 93, 96, 97 and 99, speaks of the Lord exercising his sovereignty as king over the world, and this might be connected with the renewal of life in nature which was brought by the rains at the time of the same festival. Certainly the Babylonians spoke of the gods' kingship in this connection: but there is a danger in interpreting one religion by another, and a danger in assuming that every reference to the themes of these festivals indicates that the psalm concerned was used then. We sing about Christ's resurrection at other times than Easter! Nevertheless the general point can be accepted, that we hear these psalms of praise on the lips of the congregation gathered for worship.

These gatherings were presumably not only the ones required by the temple regulations. When the people were in danger or defeated, and brought their lament to God, they no doubt gathered specially for that purpose in the temple. When their prayer was answered, they gathered there again to give God the glory.

Furthermore, what was true of the congregation was true also of the individual. The temple was the hub of Old Testament spiritual life for the individual as well as for the community, for there God had promised to dwell, there he heard prayer, there sacrifices were offered. So the individual in need came to the temple with his lament, perhaps in the company of his family and friends; and when his prayer was answered, he too returned to give God the glory before his people and to offer the sacrifice that expressed in concrete form his thanksgiving and devotion.

As we have noted, the psalms do make some specific references to their liturgical background, in the headings prefixed to nearly all of them, but the precise meaning of these headings is unclear. Perhaps this is not surprising: a future generation might make little sense of 'common metre' or 'capo on second fret'. But the areas covered by the titles are fairly clear. Some refer to the smaller collections of psalms from which the Psalter was compiled: 'The Choirmaster's', 'The Korahites'', 'Asaph's' (many individual psalms naturally featured in more than one of these collections). 'David's' is probably a similar formula: 'David's Psalms', like 'Alexander's Hymns', were not necessarily ones which he wrote himself, but ones in a collection named after him. The significance of the occasional more detailed reference to David is discussed below in connection with Psalm 51 (see p. 153).

Other titles describe the kind of psalm in some way: 'song', 'love song', 'psalm', 'maskil'. The fact that we can only transliterate rather than translate the last term illustrates what is also true of the others, that though they apparently refer to types of composition, we cannot specify what types.

A third kind of reference in the headings is perhaps to the tune or instrumentation ('according to lilies', 'according to Alamoth'); but with these and the other less frequent elements in the headings we move totally into the realm of guesswork. The same is true with the obscure word 'Selah' which recurs in the middle of some psalms. The suggestion that this was what David said when he broke a string is as plausible as any!

The Psalms as poetry

The Psalms are poetry, though they are not set out as such in the traditional versions and translations of the Old Testament. Old Testament poetry has two distinctive features, which are in fact easier to represent in translation than such marks of poetry as syllable-count or rhyme. The first is that there are a set number of stresses in each line. There can be any number of unemphasized syllables, but the number of stressed syllables generally falls into a pattern. The most common pattern is 3–3 (three stressed in each half-line):

'Purge me with hyssop, and I shall be clean;

    wash me, and I shall be whiter than snow.

Fill me with joy and gladness;

    let the bones which thou hast broken rejoice' (51:7–8, RSV).

Hebrew makes a great deal of use of compound words, and in

each of these half-lines there are, in fact, only three Hebrew words, and thus clearly three stresses.

These two verses also exemplify the other characteristic of Hebrew poetry, the phenomenon of parallelism. In each verse the second half of the line balances the first half, by repeating, amplifying, developing or contrasting with it. The whole line is thus the unit of thought, and sometimes it is important to realize this in order to understand the psalmist aright. For instance, the two elements in an expression such as 'day and night' can be separated from each other in the two halves of the line:

'By day Yahweh used to command his covenant-love,
and by night his song was with me' (42:8).

The psalmist does not mean that only by day did he know the Lord's love and that he sang his praise only at night. He means that day and night (*i.e.* continually) he experienced God's love and responded with praise.

A further consequence of the poetic nature of the Psalms is that they use imagery and symbolism more extensively than prose does. We should not be prosaic in interpreting them, therefore. When the author of Psalms 42–43 describes his affliction in terms of spiritual longing (42:1), weeping and personal insult (3), geographical isolation (6), drowning (7), mourning and oppression (9), physical attack (10) and injustice and deceit (43:1), we are not to look for one situation which might embody all these, but be open to the possibility that each of them is a poetic way of describing circumstances that are not literally described. Precisely this use of imagery, however, makes it easier for us to identify with the psalmist. He is not giving us a literal description of an experience we have not shared. He is describing what a situation felt like in terms we may only too often have used ourselves ('everything was against me', 'God seemed miles away', 'things got on top of me', 'I was overwhelmed', 'it was devastating').

The Psalms and our spirituality

Clearly there are points at which we cannot literally identify with the Psalms. They presuppose a religion centred upon a temple: we know the presence of God independently of a building. They speak for the concerns of a people with a king at its head: we have no such king, but the One who fulfilled all that the kings never lived up to. They manifest no 'sure and certain hope of the resurrection of the dead': we live the other side of that first resurrection that makes ours possible too.

Nevertheless, precisely at these points we may paradoxically experience a deep sense of identification. The material location of God's presence did not prevent its being a spiritual reality. Thus the enthusiasm and longing of the psalmist with regard to the presence of God will not be an attitude we can feel superior about. Rather it challenges us as to the reality of our own experience of God. The kingly focus of the Psalms, precisely because Jesus is the fulfilment of the kingly ideal, will speak to us of him, and also of ourselves—for have we not become 'a line of kings and priests' (Rev. 5 : 10, JB) in him? The this-worldly orientation of the Psalms starts with life as we actually live it, and reminds us that God did create this world and means it to be enjoyed; but it also brings home the real achievement of Christ's death and resurrection.

More profound, however, than these differences at surface-level between the spiritual circumstances of the psalmist and our own, is the deep underlying identity of situation. The Psalms are referred to in the New Testament more often than any other Old Testament book. The church in its worship adopted Israel's hymnbook as her own and for long used no other: in fact, the Psalms were required to be read in church more often than any book of the New Testament. Individual Christians have often possessed a copy of the New Testament bound with the Psalms and no other part of the Old Testament. They do embody the same spiritual experience as ours (or the experience we aspire to).

This identity of experience, I believe, extends even to the aspects of the Psalms that people often find offensive. Can a Christian really declare himself abandoned by God in the way the psalmist does? Can he really call down judgment on his enemies as the psalmist does? Whether or not he ought to (it is at least arguable that in the latter case the psalmist is concerned for righteousness rather than for personal vengeance), the fact is that even believers do feel that way. The presence of these prayers in the Psalter indicates at least that God gives permission for them to be prayed. What he then does with them is his business;

though we may grant that ours, in our better moments, is to recognize that these are not the profoundest moments in the Psalter (except in the sense that, in their own paradoxical way, they point towards the cross to which such human realities pushed God), and that, while they may be uttered, they may then need to be repented of (*cf.* Je. 15:15–21).

Even at this point, then, 'the Psalms speak for us', as I hope the following pages will show.

God has forgotten me
(Psalms 42 and 43)

42   *The choirmaster's.   A poem.   The Korahites'.*

¹ *Like the deer that longs for streams with water,*
  So my whole being longs for you, O God.
² *I thirst for God, for the living God:*
  When shall I come and appear in God's presence?
³ *Tears have been my food day and night*
  As people say to me continually, 'Where is your God?'
⁴ *I call to mind, as I pour out the feelings which overwhelm me,*
  How I used to make my way to God's dwelling,
  Lead them along to his house,
  With the noise of praise resounding, the festival clamour.
⁵   *Why should I be laid low and groaning in distress?*
     I must wait for God. I shall yet praise him
     For the salvation that comes from his countenance.

⁶ *My God, I am laid low. Thus I call you to mind*
  From the country of Jordan and the Hermons, from Mount Mizar.
⁷ *Deep calls to deep with the noise of your torrents;*
  All your waves break and roll over me.
⁸ *Day and night Yahweh used to show me his covenant-love;*
  I would sing his praise and pray to God who was my life.
⁹ *I will say to God, my rock, 'Why have you put me out of your mind?*
  Why must I go about in this gloomy way because of my enemies'
     oppression?'

[10] *My foes have broken me with their taunts*
As they say to me continually, 'Where is your God?'
[11] *Why should I be laid low and groaning in distress?*
I must wait for God. I shall yet praise him
As the salvation of my countenance and my God.

43

[1] *Vindicate me, O God, take up my cause against a faithless nation.*
Rescue me from men who betray and deceive.
[2] *For you are the God who is my refuge. Why have you abandoned me?*
Why must I go about in this gloomy way because of my enemies'
oppression?
[3] *Send your light and your faithfulness, let them guide me,*
Let them bring me to your holy mountain, to your dwelling.
[4] *Then I will come to God's altar, to God my joyful delight.*
I will praise you on the harp, God my God.
[5] *Why should I be laid low and groaning in distress?*
I must wait for God. I shall yet praise him
As the salvation of my countenance and my God.

One reason for the Old Testament's importance today is that it
starts from where men are. Our world has little awareness of
God, while the church and the individual Christian, too, sometimes find themselves (perhaps because they have to live in this
same world) in turn losing their awareness of God. God does not
seem to make his presence felt. He seems difficult to find.

Psalms 42 and 43, like many others, express the feelings of a
man who cannot get to God. They are really two parts of one
psalm.[1] It is a 'lament'[2]—perhaps one uttered by some individual
cut off from Jerusalem and from the people of God, perhaps one
used by the congregation as a whole in exile, or perhaps one sung
by the king at a time of national crisis.[3] We cannot be sure in what
situation it arose, but it is in the Psalter because it evidently could
be used, and was used, in many situations. The outward crisis,
whatever it was, provoked the inner crisis of which the psalm

[1] Many mss in fact join them together (*cf.* NEB, JB), and 43 has no heading of
its own. It concludes with a similar refrain to that of 42:5, 11, and its metre
and language are similar (*cf.* especially 43:2b with 42:9b).
[2] See above, pp. 17 ff.
[3] 42:4 probably indicates that the psalmist is not just a private individual
but a leader.

speaks, and with which many in quite different outward circumstances could identify.

We are used to hymns with refrains. Psalms do not usually have
them, but here is a rare example. 42:5, 42:11 and 43:5 are similar
if not identical,[4] and they apparently conclude three stanzas:
42:1–5, 42:6–11 and 43:1–5. Each of these stanzas has three
elements. In each the psalmist begins by letting himself go: he
gives expression to his feelings. In each he goes on to make himself think: he turns his mind away from the present situation. In
each, finally, in similar words he pulls himself together.

LETTING ONESELF GO

The psalmist gives expression to his feelings in the three stanzas
by drawing three pictures of himself: 'I'm parched' (42:1–3);
'I'm overwhelmed' (42:6–7, 9–10); 'I'm misjudged' (43:1–2).

'I'm parched' (42:1–3)

In Britain, we generally take rain for granted and long for the
sun. Sun is good news; rain is bad news (or no news). In Palestine,
the reverse is broadly true. The sun is a danger (cf. Ps. 121:6;
Is. 49:10; Jon. 4:8). From May to September it beats down
ceaselessly and bakes the land. There is no rain and there are very
few rivers that flow all the year round. The great cities of ancient
times, such as Megiddo and Hazor, had elaborate water systems
to conserve supplies during this annual drought, but even these
tend to run dry as summer wears on. The climate is all right for a
camel, with its built-in water conservation equipment. It is tor-
ture for *the deer that longs for streams with water*, when all it can find
is the characteristic Palestinian dry river beds that flow only in
winter. It strains its head for the smell or the sound of running
water.

> The soil is parched,
> the dykes are dry,
> the granaries are deserted,
> the barns ruinous;
> for the rains have failed.
> The cattle are exhausted,

[4] See the comments below, p. 43.

the herds of oxen distressed
because they have no pasture;
the flocks of sheep waste away. . . .
The very cattle in the field look up to thee;
for the water-channels are dried up,
and fire has devoured the open pastures.

(Joel 1:17–18, 20, NEB)

Their flock-masters send their boys for water;
they come to the pools but find no water there. . . .
The hind calves in the open country
and forsakes her young
because there is no grass;
for lack of herbage, wild asses stand in the high bare places
and snuff the wind for moisture,
as wolves do, and their eyes begin to fail.

(Je. 14:3, 5–6, NEB)

And that is how I feel myself in relation to God, the psalmist declares: *my whole being*[5] *longs for you, O God. I thirst for God*[6] (1b, 2a).

Given the importance of rain in Palestine, and the people's awareness that it cannot be taken for granted, it is not surprising that river and stream, fountain and well, spring and shower, are images applied to God. He alone is 'the fountain of living water' (Je. 17:13). He gives his people water from his 'river of delights' and with him is 'the fountain of life' (Ps. 36:8, 9). Thus Psalm 42 speaks of thirsting for *the living God*[7] (*cf.* 84:2), who is that spring

---

[5] This phrase from NEB expresses the meaning of *nepeš* (traditionally 'soul') as well as any English translation can. The word does not refer to 'soul' as opposed to 'body': the 'persons' born of Jacob (*e.g.* Ex. 1:5) and the 'creatures' made by God (*e.g.* Gn. 1:20) were definitely flesh and blood. 'Person' and 'self' are the nearest single English words. The Old Testament does not make the sharp distinction between 'soul' and 'body' that is often characteristic of Western thinking (under Greek influence). Certainly when it speaks of a man's 'soul' it generally implies a reference to his inner being, to what makes him tick. Nevertheless, it thinks of the latter as receiving outward expression in the person he shows himself to be.

[6] *Cf.* Ps. 63:1, where a similar longing is expressed.

[7] *The lively God* might convey better the atmosphere of the expression. Asserting that Yahweh is the living God suggests that he is active and powerful. He is no inactive, dead idol, but a being who makes his person and his presence felt (see, *e.g.*, Dt. 5:26; Jos. 3:10; Je. 10:10).

of living water, and who alone can quench a man's thirst. Thus the psalmist asks, *When*[8] *shall I come and appear in God's presence?* (2b).

Coming to God's presence involves coming to the temple, for it is his house, his dwelling (42:4; 43:3). It is where he lives. The picture is quite a down-to-earth one. If you want to see a man, you go to his house. If you want to see God, you go to his.

It was, of course, realized in Israel that the notion of God dwelling on earth was an extraordinary one. Heaven, indeed 'the highest heaven', could not contain him; much less a mere material building (1 Ki. 8:27). This psalm itself gives paradoxical testimony to the awareness that he was accessible anywhere, in the fact that the psalmist speaks with God even as he laments God's inaccessibility. The qualification for meeting God was moral rather than geographical (*cf.* Is. 57:15; 66:1–2).

And yet mankind has a deep need for holy places. Even Christians today are inclined to call their church building 'God's house', despite the fact that the New Testament speaks in another way altogether (*cf.* 1 Cor. 3:16; 6:19). Under the old covenant God condescended to this need and allowed Solomon to build him a house, and there he deigned to dwell. There he met with his people, there he spoke to them, there the events of Israel's redemption were commemorated (*cf.* Ps. 42:4). From there came God's revelation, there sacrifices were made and men were assured that their sins were forgiven (*cf.* 43:3–4). There prayers were offered and answers promised, and praise returned when the answers became experienced realities (*cf.* 42:8; 43:4). The temple meant almost everything. It was the very heart of the people's life with God.

But among the uncertainties about the origin of Psalms 42 and 43, one thing is unquestionable: the writer is cut off from the temple. The reason for this we do not know, but its implication is clear: he is thereby in a real sense cut off from God's presence. He has no access to the place of word and sacrament, of praise and prayer. *When shall I come and appear in God's presence?* (2b). *Tears have been my food day and night* (3a). I have not eaten, only wept and wept in my distress. And all I get is the added hurt of

[8] A key word in the laments as they ask, 'Lord, *when* are you going to answer?' (*e.g.* Pss. 101:2; 119:82, 84). *Cf.* the question 'how long?' in others (*e.g.* Pss. 6:3; 74:10; 80:4; 90:13; 94:3).

the taunt of the mockers, *as people say to me continually, 'Where is your God?'* (3b). The words recall Elijah's taunting of Baal prophets with the possibility that their unresponsive God might be asleep, or in the toilet (1 Ki. 18:26–27). But the boot is here on the other foot. *'Where is your God?'* The words bite into the psalmist because they verbalize the question he is asking himself. Is Yahweh powerless? Or does he not care? Where is he? My inability to reach him is destroying me. *I pour out the feelings which overwhelm me* (4).[9] These words prepare us for the image that dominates the next stanza.

'I'm overwhelmed' (42:6–7, 9–10)

I am laid low,[1] the psalmist begins, describing his downcastness with a phrase similar to ones that have occurred in the first stanza (4–5). But the image that dominates the second stanza is very different from that of the first. You might say it was contradictory, if you were being prosaic. The psalmist pictures himself at Israel's northernmost extremity: *I call you to mind from the country of Jordan and the Hermons, from Mount Mizar* (6).[2] Perhaps he was literally there and unable to get south to Judaea for some reason. For the later reader, however, the location is a symbol of isolation from the place of God's dwelling.

In the winter the rains cascade down the hillside of the Hermon range, and even in the height of summer the snows from the top peaks are still seeping through on such a large scale as to feed magnificent waterfalls at the Jordan headwaters near Dan and what was later known as Caesarea Philippi. The crashing of the

[9] More literally, 'I pour out my soul on myself' (*cf.* Jb. 30:16). The idea seems to be that the self is overcome by feelings that are part of it yet in some way distinguishable from it and acting upon it (*cf.* BDB, p. 753b).

[1] More literally, 'my soul prostrates itself upon me'; *cf.* the previous footnote. The picture is of the 'soul' bent double upon itself; perhaps one can compare this with the downcast, turned-in-on-himself bearing that often characterizes the depressed person.

[2] The geographical references raise difficulties. The identity of Mount Hermon is certain enough, though the plural occurs only here; presumably the reference is to the mountain's several peaks or to the range in general. *The country of Jordan* presumably refers to the river's headwaters in the Hermon area, though this is not explicit. *Mizar* comes from a root meaning 'little', and JB takes it to refer to the 'little hill' of Zion which is worth more than impressive Hermon (*cf.* Ps. 68:15–16). More likely it is another straightforward but now unlocatable geographical reference.

waters suggests the second image that describes how the psalmist feels: 'I'm overwhelmed' (7). It is not a random poetic symbol. Throughout the ancient Near East this crashing of waters is a potent symbol of the powers of chaos, and the Bible often alludes to this way of thinking. Creation involved the separating of the waters and the providing of a vault to restrain the waters above (Gn. 1:6–7; *cf.* Ps. 104:5–9). The flood meant the breaking through of the springs of the great abyss (Gn. 7:11). The beasts in Daniel's vision arose from the great sea (Dn. 7:2–3). In John's vision of the new world the sea is no more (Rev. 21:1). The awesome power of the crashing waters speaks of the power of chaos asserting itself against cosmos, the power of evil asserting itself against God. For the individual, this power is represented by death, which ever reaches out into life and seeks to overwhelm man in its waves and torrents and floods (*cf.* 2 Sa. 22:5, 17[3]). Being in mortal danger (physical or spiritual) is like drowning (*cf.* Ps. 69:1–2), and it is 'out of the depths' (130:1) that the psalmist prays for the Lord's deliverance. So here: *Deep calls to deep with the noise of your torrents; all your waves break and roll over me*[4] (7). I am overwhelmed. I am crushed. I am drowning. I desperately need something to hold on to, a rock to cling to, to save me from the flood.

The idea of God being our *rock* (9), the rock who saves us,[5] gains extra force from (if it does not have its origin in) the flood image: 'I thought you were that rock, but you have failed me.' *I will say to God, my rock, 'Why have you put me out of your mind*[6]?

[3] *Cf.* also Jonah's psalm (Jon. 2): it has in mind not merely his physical experience of being thrown into the sea, but more the theological symbolism of that experience. The sea is the very embodiment of the forces of chaos and death.

[4] More literally, 'all your breakers and rollers pass over me'.

[5] It is regrettable that such expressions as 'the rock of our salvation' continue to appear in modern translations, as they are a misleadingly literalist way of rendering a Hebrew idiom. Hebrew makes less use of adjectives than English does, and often prefers to link two nouns. We do, of course, sometimes do this in English (*cf.* such expressions as 'a tower of strength', 'a city of importance'). In Hebrew, when pronouns need to be added to the expression, grammatically they have to be affixed to the second noun, though logically they may belong at least as much to the first. Thus 'the God of our salvation' is 'our saving God' or 'our God who saves us' (*e.g.* Ps. 68:19).

[6] More literally, 'forgotten'; but Jews even before Freud knew that forgetting implies allowing something to go out of your mind and neglecting it (*cf.*

Why[7] . . .?' (9). Again the words recall a time when the boot was on the other foot. In Isaiah 40–46, Yahweh issues challenge after challenge to the so-called gods of the Babylonians. 'Is there a God besides me?' he asks. 'There is no Rock; I know not any' (Is. 44:8). 'There is only one Rock,' says Yahweh. 'Where has he gone, then?' ask the mockers. Like the island of Atlantis, he seems to have sunk without trace.

'*I'm misjudged*' (43:1–2)

In the first stanza the psalmist referred briefly to the attacks of men who keep asking, 'Where is your God?' (42:3). He described these at greater length in the second stanza (42:9–10), and the third takes up again where the previous one left off. The attacks of the mockers now come into the centre of the picture.

Vindicate me, O God, take up my cause against a faithless nation (1a). The psalmist uses words that belong in the lawcourt. We are probably not to infer that he is formally on trial; informally he is, however. People whom he ought to be able to rely on[8] bring taunts rather than comfort. Their word cannot, after all, be trusted. So, he pleads, *rescue me from men who betray and deceive* (1b).

Why? The question comes again. *Why must I go about in this gloomy way*[9] *because of my enemies' oppression?* (2b). Here he picks up

---

Pss. 10:12; 44:17; 74:19), as remembering implies bringing to mind and taking care of (*cf.* Pss. 88:5; 103:18; 137:7). See B. S. Childs, *Memory and Tradition in Israel* (SCM Press, 1962), especially p. 34.

[7] Like 'when' and 'how long', *why* is a key word in the laments (*e.g.* Pss. 10:1; 22:1; 44:24; as well as 43:2 below). Unlike 'when', however, it receives no answer (*cf.* Job). Perhaps it is anyway 'not so much a demand for explanation as an expression of perplexity' (Anderson).

[8] This is suggested by the expression translated *faithless, i.e.* not *ḥāsîḏ. ḥeseḏ* is a key Hebrew noun denoting the keeping of commitments, the fulfilling of obligations that have been undertaken (see below, on 51:1). *ḥāsîḏ* is an adjective derived from this noun: it describes the person who does keep his commitment. In the Bible, it seems only to be used of the relationship between God and man, with reference to God's loyalty to man (*e.g.* Ps. 18:25; Je. 3:12, RSV 'merciful') and to man's loyalty to God (*e.g.* Pss. 18:25; 32:6); thus in Ps. 43:1 it suggests that they are not merely being unfaithful to him but also to God. In Maccabaean times and since, the *ḥᵃsîḏîm* are the especially orthodox Jews.

[9] EVV 'mourning': a mourner took on a dark and dishevelled appearance as an outward sign of his grief (*cf.* 1 Sa. 4:12; 2 Sa. 12:20; Jb. 30:28; Je. 6:26). No doubt the word was then used metaphorically of gloom, as here.

the complaint he had expressed in the previous stanza (42:9). Why does he have to put up with the mockery that hurts like a physical assault (10)?[1] Not only does his own misery oppress him; his foes' taunts bow him down physically too. He is a broken man.

The psalmist is in the classic position of a Jeremiah or a Job, men attacked in God's name by God's servants or their own friends. These are people he should have been able to rely on; they owe it to God to live like God's people. But they behave like one of the heathen nations, like a race of gentiles (43:1).[2]

Some commentators perceive in the psalm as the stanzas develop a deepening calm and trust on the psalmist's part. He becomes assured of God's presence (42:8), he prays more explicitly (43:1, 3–4). Even if this is so,[3] at the same time as the stanzas develop the screw gets tighter, the agony deeper. At first it was 'I can't get to God' (42:1–2); then 'God has forgotten me' (42:9); now 'God has abandoned me' (43:2). 'He has not just overlooked me. He has cast me off, rejected me, and that against the background of my having made him *my refuge*[4] (a similar metaphor to that of the rock). I could, after all, have looked elsewhere. I could have made human resources my refuge (*cf.* Is. 30:2) or other gods my rock (*cf.* Dt. 32:30–31). There are other places to get water (to revert to an earlier metaphor). But I knew that they were mere cisterns, at best capable of storing water (but not of producing

---

[1] More literally, 'with murder in my bones my foes taunt me'. But 'bones' can stand for the whole person (*e.g.* Ps. 35:10, they praise God; Is. 66:14, they flourish). It is often difficult in the Psalms, and in passages such as Is. 53 and the 'confessions' of Jeremiah which are influenced by them, to be sure what is literal and what is metaphorical in the description of distress. Is the psalmist physically ill? Or is he under physical attack? Is he literally in northern Galilee? Is he literally on trial? Or are all these metaphors for depression, isolation, mockery and slander? Perhaps the situation varies with different psalms (and different recensions of the same psalm).

[2] *Nation* (*gôy*) most often refers to a gentile people; thus the word is probably pejorative here. The implication that Israelites are behaving like unbelievers is perhaps also made by 42:3, 10, for the question 'Where is your God?' appears characteristically on heathen lips (*cf.* Pss. 79:10; 115:2); Israelites, indeed, speak this way at the cross (Mt. 27:43).

[3] On 42:8, see below, however; and it is quite usual for the actual prayers in a lament to become more explicit nearer the end.

[4] A stronghold or fortress that provides security and safety from enemy attack (Jdg. 6:26; Is. 23:11, 14).

it), and in fact cracked and incapable even of that; and I knew that you were the only spring of living water (Je. 2:13). But the spring seems to have run dry, like a brook that is not to be trusted, whose waters fail (Je. 15:18). I knew you threatened such an experience for those who persist in looking elsewhere (Am. 8:11–13). But I have not looked elsewhere. I came to you as my refuge, my hiding-place; and you shut the door and left me at the mercy of my pursuers. *Why?* (42:9a). *Why?* (42:9b). *Why?* (43:2a). *Why?* (43:2b).'

Prayer in the absence of God

Having reviewed the sections in which the psalmist lets himself go and gives expression to what he feels, we may note certain lessons for ourselves. First, that prayer does mean getting things off our chest. Psychology has given us clearer insight into the consequences of bottling things up inside, though no doubt men have always been aware of these (*cf.* Ps. 32:3–4; Je. 20:9). Psalmists and prophets do not repress their feelings. One of the features of the psalms that often causes offence is their open desire for vengeance on their enemies. Now there are various ways of mitigating the apparent vindictiveness of these prayers,[5] but if the feelings *are* personal, then perhaps these prayers reflect the fact that such feelings are better expressed in some way than repressed. The psalmist has his longings and his frustrations, his distress and his hurt, his resentment and his anger; he does not hide them.

And it is before God that he gives expression to them. This is not merely an emotional catharsis, like crying one's heart out in an empty room, or losing one's temper and taking it out on the cushions. It is more adult to say what one feels to the person one regards as responsible, and the psalmist is not afraid to do that. He does not seem to hesitate to be quite straight with God. He assumes that God is big enough to take it and loving enough to absorb it. He is honest to God. So often he reminds us of Job. Now Job was rebuked for demanding that all the secrets of the universe be explained to him. But he was commended for refusing to take the easy way out and confess his sins as his friends urged, for insisting that he had done nothing to deserve such affliction as he had received and that the situation imperilled any

[5] *Cf.* above, pp. 23 f.

coherent understanding of the relationship between God and man (Jb. 42:7). He had been honest to God.[6]

Thirdly, we may note for our own encouragement that the experience of God's absence does not paralyse prayer. Paradoxically, it prompts prayer. The temple is the house of prayer (Is. 56:7) and the psalmist is cut off from it. He cannot get to the place where God deigns to be with his people. He does not feel the presence of God. Yet this makes his prayer more urgent, not less so. In contrast, often the feeling that God has let us down and abandoned us, that we cannot experience his presence or get through to him, causes people to abandon prayer, to stop trying to find God again. For calling on in such times we need to store in our bank of spiritual resources the example of the psalmist, that prayer is still possible when God seems to be absent.

Fourthly, we may infer that, for the psalmist and for us, this possibility is open because trouble and deprivation come with God's knowledge and according to his will, not by his oversight or weakness. The point is made most clear by the unobtrusive pronouns of 42:7: the floods that threaten to overwhelm are *your* torrents, *your* breakers, *your* rollers (*cf.* 88:6–7). In the myths of other ancient Near Eastern peoples, the powers of chaos threaten and overcome even the gods; the myths no doubt thus reflect a deep insecurity in the world, a deep uncertainty as to the stability of human life, on the part of those who narrated and believed them. But the Old Testament believes that 'Yahweh sits enthroned over the flood' (Ps. 29:10) and that his lordship cannot be broken. Of course, actual experience of life in Israel included many troubles, as it did in Babylon or Canaan, but these were interpreted as within Yahweh's control and subject to his will. The powers of chaos will not win the victory. They have been dethroned in creation and history.

At first sight the belief that God is behind the trouble that comes to us is a frightening doctrine: what kind of a God is this, whose purpose includes so much distress? But the alternative—a God whose purpose is continually being frustrated by evil—is even more frightening. Better a God whose mystery we cannot understand (but who has given us grounds for trusting when we cannot understand) than one whose adequacy we cannot rely on, or whose interest we cannot be sure of.

[6] See further, on Ps. 44:9–16, below, pp. 58 ff.

For even God's hostility is a mark of his involvement. Children are alleged to like being chastised by their parents: at least their action shows that they are interested. Even God's rejection is an indication that he bothers. It provides a basis for conversation. It is one better than being ignored.

MAKING ONESELF THINK

Although the psalmist does not hesitate to let himself go, he knows when enough is enough. The expression of grief can become indulgence in grief. In each stanza he moves on, to turn his mind away from his distress. There is a pattern here. The life of faith (or of unfaith, for that matter) involves a right relationship of heart, mind and will. In the psalmist's situation, the feelings of the heart cry out for expression and they must receive it. But there must come a time when the mind is applied to the situation too, for this is the way of renewal (*cf*. Rom. 12:2). So he makes himself think, reminds himself of other realities than his present distress: corporate worship in the past (42:4); personal experience of God's grace (42:8); renewed worship in the future (43:3-4).

Corporate worship in the past (42:4)

I call to mind . . . how I used to make my way to God's dwelling, lead them along to his house. I cannot do this now, but I recall when I could. The calling to mind was, no doubt, a bitter-sweet experience. In as far as it means recalling what he is missing, it would be an aggravation of his distress. But at the same time it might alleviate his distress, in as far as he is reminding himself that this present deprivation is not permanent. It had a before, and (as we shall see later) it will have an after. So he recalls the wondrous joy, the enthusiastic, ecstatic praise which he had shared with God's people in the festival procession, *with the noise of praise resounding, the festival clamour.* Anyone who has experienced the 'festivals of praise' and the like which have been held in recent years will know something of the psalmist's exultation, and will perhaps have found (as he does) that those moments of being uplifted in the praise of God can continue to provide spiritual nourishment long after the event itself is over. And he could not buy the LP!

The festival can function this way partly because the actual event is not merely a subjective experience. Behind the recollection of the festival of praise is what the festival stood for, the salvation events, the exodus and the covenant which it commemorated. We have noted that the temple was at the centre of the relationship between God and his people. Now the temple was in use every day. But there were certain great pilgrim feasts each year when even its worship rose to a higher plane. At Passover and Unleavened Bread in the spring, at Pentecost in high summer, and at Tabernacles in the autumn at the end of the year, the facts of God's creation and redemption, his lordship and his covenant, were brought home to his people in the deepest way. The psalmist thus reminds himself of the acts of God which still form the basis of faith, even though he personally cannot join in their commemoration in the place where his fellows enjoy the fruit of them and where they experience the presence of the God who made himself known to Israel in those events. Those objective realities are still objective realities. The question verbalized by his foes but latent in his own heart—'*Where is your God?*' Has he any power? Does he care? (*cf.* verse 3, just previously to the recalling of verse 4)—receives its answer in this reminder of objective realities, of creation and history.

Personal experience of God's grace (42:8)

The remembering of 42:4 was a recalling of an event; now the psalmist turns his mind more specifically to remembering God himself (6), seeking by this means to bridge the distance that separates him from God. He recalls his individual enjoyment of the Lord's love,[7] his personal life of praise and prayer, the fact that God *was* his life.[8] He refers to a day-and-night (in other words, continual) experience of God's grace, which contrasts with the day-and-night fasting and weeping of his distress (3).

The combination of corporate worship (4) and personal piety (8) as elements in the psalmist's spirituality deserves note. Often these two have been regarded as mutually exclusive alternatives. Old Testament study itself has sometimes assumed that one or other is *the* central feature of Old Testament faith at its most

[7] *ḥesed* again; *cf.* above, on 43:1, and below, on 51:1.
[8] The expression *God* (who is) *my life* parallels that of the next line (9a), *God* (who is) *my rock*, and also the one in 43:2, *God* (who is) *my refuge*. *Cf.* Dahood

authentic, or that corporate religion characterized the period before the exile, with individualism coming only later. But both belong to biblical religion from beginning to end. Of course different periods may manifest an emphasis on one or other: the balance is a difficult one to keep. The evangelical tradition, for instance, has overemphasized the individual, and is rediscovering corporate piety: indeed, the pendulum may be swinging too far, and a Jeremiah or an Ezekiel may soon be needed to remind us that each of us stands as an individual before God. There is a balance to keep here, and the psalmist again models it with his awareness of the reality of corporate worship, but also of the reality of individual experience of God.[9]

There is one difficulty about understanding the experience he is referring to, however. The English translations vary widely in their renderings of 42:8, disagreeing as to how the verbs are to be taken. Is the psalmist describing how things are for him in the present, affirming that God's love and praise are real to him now (*cf.* RSV, NEB)? It seems unlikely that he could be speaking so affirmatively when he feels overwhelmed in the previous verse and forgotten in the verse that follows. The statement in fact looks more like a contrast with his present experience. It could be a prayer, *may Yahweh command his love* (JB), or a statement of confidence about the future which he believes will put right the past, *the* LORD *will command his lovingkindness* (AV). Either offers a good parallel to the prayer and expectation he expresses later (43:3-4). But there is a further possibility, that he is again contrasting the present with the past, with how things used to be (*cf.* PBV), and this suggestion commends itself because the expression is parallel with one used not long before. *I call to mind . . . how I used to make my way to God's dwelling . . .* (4); *I call you to mind . . . day and night Yahweh[1] used to show me his covenant-love; I would sing his*

---

[9] Anderson suggests, however, that this verse too may refer to a festival. Even if so, its personal meaning for the psalmist himself is emphasized by the pronouns.

[1] The personal name of the God of Israel occurs here. It is not generally used in Pss. 42–83, and a comparison of 53 with 14 and of 70 with 40:13–17 (where in each case the same verses recur) suggests that on many occasions *Yahweh* has been replaced by the general word for 'God', *'elōhîm* (hence Pss. 42–83 are called the elohistic psalter). One can imagine that in the present psalm 43:4 once ended *Yahweh my God*, and perhaps *Yahweh* occurred in 42:1, 2, 4, 5, 11; 43:1, 5, as Kraus suggests. The same possibility obtains

praise and pray to God who was my life (6, 8).[2] As in the previous
stanza, the psalmist turns his mind back to his experience in the
past, but now he recalls explicitly what God's grace meant to him
as an individual. He *had* known God's covenant-faithfulness, he
had been a man of praise and prayer, God *had* been his life. The
memory stimulates a prayer that God may return to him (8c–9),
which is developed in the final stanza.

Renewed worship in the future (43:3–4)

Near the close of the psalm attention is turned away from the past
and the experience that the psalmist now misses, to the future and
the anticipation of that experience being restored. *Then I will come
to God's altar, to God my joyful delight;*[3] *I will praise you on the harp,
God my God* (4). The psalmist longs to experience again that of
which he allows himself his bitter-sweet recollection. He is doing
his best to cope with being cut off from the temple and its worship, from the altar and its offerings. But he cannot be content
with this situation, and longs to get back there.

We have noted the importance of putting a right evaluation on
both corporate and individual worship. Here we are again re-

---

sometimes in the rest of the psalms we shall consider. The preference for
'God' rather than *Yahweh* may have been based in a concern about the danger
of taking Yahweh's name 'in vain' (Ex. 20:7); people therefore avoided
taking it on their lips at all. In the light of this, in 42:8 the presence of *Yahweh*
is surprising. Perhaps the psalm was revised after its first inclusion in the
elohistic psalter. The variants shown by psalms that occur twice (*e.g.* the ones
mentioned above) show that such revision went on (as it does with our
hymns).

[2] To a Westerner it is puzzling that the same verb can be interpreted by
different translations as future, precative, present or past. Hebrew, however,
has only two tenses, and even they are not tenses. The *perfect* is fairly straightforward: it generally refers to actions which have already happened. It thus
corresponds to an English simple past (past historic/aorist) or perfect (or
future perfect). The *imperfect* includes actions which do, will, should, could,
might or used to happen, and can thus be equivalent to present, future,
optative, subjunctive or imperfect. All the finite verbs in 2b and 4 are imperfect; EVV regularly translate them as future (2b), present (4a) and past (4b)

[3] More literally, 'the joy of my delight'. Hebrew has no special forms to
express comparatives and superlatives, and for the latter it repeats nouns, as
in such expressions as 'holy of holies', 'king of kings', 'song of songs'. The
two nouns are usually identical, but they can be merely synonymous (*cf.* GK
133, i).

minded of the importance of the former. Under the new covenant, as under the old, the gathering of God's people is *the* place where he is to be praised and glorified, where testimony is to be given to him,[4] and the ministry of word and sacrament is *the* regular means of grace (see, for instance, 1 Cor. 11–14; Col. 3:16; Heb. 10:19–25). Calvin infers that the psalmist's example here 'may well suffice to put to shame the arrogance of those who without concern can bear to be deprived of those means, or rather, who proudly despise them, as if it were in their power to ascend to heaven in a moment's flight'. They are a ladder by which we, who lack wings, may nevertheless reach God—although, Calvin adds, they are only a ladder, and not the reality to which the ladder leads.[5]

But in order to get to the place of worship, the psalmist has to be brought in from his present wilderness. *Send your light and your faithfulness, let them guide me, let them bring me to your holy mountain, to your dwelling* (3). Earlier he was looking back on the festivals which recalled (foundationally among the other salvation events) Yahweh's achievement on Israel's behalf at the exodus. In the present what he needs, in effect, is a new experience of the exodus realities. From Egypt Israel had journeyed with the leading of Yahweh's presence in the pillar of cloud by day, and with the light of his presence in the pillar of fire by night (Ex. 13:21). From Sinai she had been blessed by Aaron with the light of Yahweh's countenance, with his grace and peace (Nu. 6:22–27). Her liberation from Egypt had as its objective from the first her worshipping in Yahweh's presence (*cf.* Ex. 3:12, 18; 5:1), and the narrative of the exodus leads to the building of God's tabernacle at Sinai (Ex. 35–40). His coming to dwell there proves that he had brought her from Egypt and that this was his purpose in doing so (Ex. 29:43–46). On a broader canvas, the whole journey finds its climax not just in the conquest of the land but in the building of God's dwelling on Zion, and this objective, too, is in mind from the first (*cf.* Ex. 15:13–17).

The psalmist looks forward to recapitulating in his own experience liberation from bondage and escort to the place of

---

[4] The verb translated *praise* means more strictly 'acknowledge', 'confess', 'testify to'; *cf.* on 49:18, below, p. 136.

[5] From Calvin's comments on 42:1.

God's presence by God's own guides.[6] He cannot get back to God's presence, but he relies on God to get him back there in God's time. God's rejection of him will not be the end. He will get there. *I will come . . . to God my joyful delight.*

PULLING ONESELF TOGETHER

In each stanza, then, the psalmist first lets himself go and gives expression to his feelings. Then he makes himself think, turning his mind from his present trouble to his past and future experience of communal worship and personal nearness to God. He reflects the double bipolarity of living: present and future, present and past.

But then the third element in each stanza is the refrain which seeks to resolve the tension between these first two. The psalmist exhorts himself to let his awareness of the past and his hope for the future determine his attitude in the present. He argues with himself and pulls himself together: *Why[7] should I be laid low and groaning in distress? I must wait for God* (42:5, 11; 43:5).[8] There is summarized the psalmist's inner feeling of brokenness, expressed outwardly in a wretched groan. From one viewpoint the misery is natural and its outward expression is right and necessary. But he cannot stop there, for both can be remedied.

I must wait for God. He summons himself to a new inward attitude. The idea of waiting for God is an important one in the Bible. It does not refer to waiting *on* God in prayer and meditation. It is not an attitude that means shutting one's eyes. On the contrary, it involves opening them wide, straining them (*cf.* Ps.

[6] God's *light* and *faithfulness* are almost personified as his guides sent out by him; *cf.* his covenant-love commissioned by him in Ps. 42:8 (the verb there is *ṣiwwāh,* 'to command') and his angels in Ps. 91:11 (also the personifications in 85:9–13; 89:14; and the less welcome ones in 55:9–11). God's light and faithfulness suggest an illumination of the way which is consistent and can be relied on.

[7] NEB takes this as an exclamatory *mah,* but these are rarer than the interrogative (other EVV), and the strong contrast in the next line (*I must wait for God*—NEB adds *yet* gratuitously) also makes the latter more likely here. The psalmist's arguing with himself is in fact a key feature of the verse.

[8] More literally, 'why are you laid low, my "soul", and groaning upon me? Wait for God'. *Cf.* 42:4 and 6, either side of the first occurrence of the refrain, with the comments above on the meaning of 'soul' and on the concept of the feelings overwhelming the self.

69:3) as one looks expectantly for God to act; in fact, it is not merely an inward attitude, though it begins as that. It is a cast of life. Waiting means hoping: not taking up a vaguely hopeful, optimistic approach to life, but looking expectantly for specific events which there is reason for believing will materialize.[9] 'Those who wait for Yahweh shall renew their strength' (Is. 40:31) means that those who are looking expectantly for the act of God which is round the corner will find that this hope gives them new strength now. The psalmist knows this truth. He knows that he will be able to keep going if he can live in hope. Where there is hope, there is life.

The new attitude can then be complemented by a new outward expression of what lies inside his spirit. *I shall again praise him* (RSV); or *I will praise him continually* (NEB). These two slightly different translations of the next phrase are both possible and could both be paralleled elsewhere in the Psalms. Both express the conviction that the praise he had rejoiced to give before (42:4, 8) and pleads for the opportunity to give again (43:4) will in fact be possible. The former translation suggests that, while the psalmist can at the moment express only distress, he looks forward to the time when his expectation is fulfilled, his waiting over: and then you listen to the praise! The psalms of lament often include a vow of praise in which the psalmist commits himself to and looks forward to coming back to say thankyou to God for what he has done.[1] He will give his public testimony to God's grace and power. His worship of God will thus be at the same time his witness to God: it is the occasion when 'those who have been redeemed by Yahweh say so' (Ps. 107:2). Praise will then celebrate what sight sees. And in the meantime faith bridges the gap between prayer and its answer, and looks forward to praise.

If the alternative translation is right, however, faith bridges that gulf in an even more spectacular way. *I will wait for God; I will praise him continually* (NEB): that is, starting now. Many laments in the Psalter do turn to praise before they finish (*e.g.* 54:6–7; 69:30–36): perhaps the transition reflects the ministry of

[9] The words for 'wait' or 'hope' cover waiting on the words of someone who was about to speak (Jb. 29:21, 23) or on the arrival of someone who was due to come (1 Sa. 10:8; 13:8), as well as on Yahweh's action in redemption (La. 3:21–24; Ps. 38:15) and on the fulfilment of his word (Ps. 119:74, 81).

[1] *E.g.* Pss. 51:13–15; 79:13.

some priest or prophet who declared a word of grace that assured the suppliant that his prayer had been heard.[2] On the basis of this word, the man in need could then begin praising God for the answer to his prayer. Or perhaps prayer itself brought the conviction that the problem had been passed on to Yahweh and was sure of his attention. Either way, faith makes it possible to say thankyou before one experiences the answer, because it brings the conviction that one *will* receive what has been requested: faith 'gives substance to our hopes' (Heb. 11:1, NEB). If we can start praising God even in trouble, and not just when it is past, then we will find that trouble itself is transformed—or rather we are transformed in it.[3]

Perhaps as much is implied by the last phrase of the refrain: *I shall praise him continually for the salvation*[4] *that comes from his countenance* (42:5)—that is, his presence.[5] When Yahweh's countenance[6] shines on his people, they are saved (Ps. 80:3, 7, 19). The face or presence of God means grace and peace (Nu. 6:25–26; *cf.* Pss. 4:6; 44:3; Is. 63:9). When Yahweh hides his face, as he has been doing, it is like being forgotten or abandoned (*cf.* Pss. 42:2, 9; 43:2), and it issues in distress and oppression. Thus the laments characteristically plead first for God to turn his face to

[2] *Cf.* Mowinckel, I, pp. 217–219. Isaiah's responses to Hezekiah's prayers in Is. 37–38 would then illustrate this phenomenon.

[3] See Merlin Carothers, *Prison to Praise* (Hodder, 1972) and other books.

[4] The word used here ($y^e\check{s}\hat{u}^c\bar{a}b$) often suggests a readiness and capacity to respond to someone's plea and to intervene on his behalf when he is in need. These aspects of the word's meaning fit the psalmist's situation: his distress, his oppression, his pleading, his hoping. *Salvation* is God's meeting of his need.

[5] The refrain in 42:5 (literally '. . . I will praise him (for) the salvation of his countenance'; 'God', which follows, is then connected with the beginning of the next verse) is slightly different from that of 42:11 and 43:5. The difference arises only from the way the Hebrew words are divided, and EVV (with the older versions and some Hebrew MSS) assimilate 42:5 to the later verses; the metre is then more even. But the refrains in the Psalms often manifest variations (see, *e.g.*, Ps. 49, discussed below), and it is worth looking at the text as it stands, particularly as the expression in 42:5 takes up the longing of 42:2. *Cf.* my article to appear in the *Jewish Quarterly Review* in 1978.

[6] Speaking about God's 'face' is a way of referring to his 'presence' or his 'person' generally—to himself as he reveals his attitude in the way that one's face does. Thus EVV often do not translate it directly: for instance, the word 'before' in EVV usually represents a Hebrew expression which could be more literally translated 'to the face of'.

us, and then for him to raise his arm on our behalf. This is *the salvation that comes from his countenance* to which the psalmist looks forward. But because he looks forward to it and moulds his attitudes by it, he will find the affliction itself transformed and will experience something of that salvation before its time.

And this experience will also affect his own face: *I shall praise him as the salvation of my countenance and my God* (42:11; 43:5). His face has looked imploringly to Yahweh; he believes Yahweh will not spurn it (*cf.* Ps. 132:10), but in response will turn his own face to look on the psalmist with favour (*cf.* Ps. 84:9). And that experience will mean the salvation of his countenance. God is the one who saves your face, who restores its smile. What lies inside a man is reflected by his face. Distress or anxiety or hostility show there. Faith, hope, anticipatory praise transform the face. Frank Lake emphasizes this theme in his consideration of Psalms 42–43 as it applies to the depressed person. The psalmist 'is looking forward to a "face to face" meeting with God. The secret of his deliverance will be an encounter between two countenances, God's and his own . . . We see how God relates us to Himself by the love in His eyes, as He looks at us in the face of His Son Jesus Christ. It is the upturned eyes of the man of faith, who, in spite of sins and sufferings, looks expectantly for the appearance of the One he still confidently calls "my God" which enables him to retain the initiative and live actively through his depression, so as to make creative use of its evil.'[7]

So the psalmist lets himself go; then he makes himself think; and thirdly he pulls himself together, talks himself into the attitude of hope and praise instead of misery and groaning. He does this not just once but three times. There is apparently no permanent resolution of the conflict inside him, which is a continuing reality that he has to keep fighting with.[8] He keeps going down, but each time he fights his way back and refuses to give in. He carries on wrestling: 'I will not let you go, unless you bless me' (Gn. 32:26).

[7] Frank Lake, *Clinical Theology* (Darton, Longman and Todd, 1966), p. 184; see further pp. 181–186 (reprinted from the Clinical Theology Association booklet *Depression*, 1965).

[8] *Cf.* Jeremiah, whose laments end on the gloomiest note (Je. 20:7–18), and Paul, who speaks of carrying in the body the death of Jesus as a lifelong experience (see 2 Cor. 4:7–12).

IN THE ABSENCE OF OUR GOD

The psalmist was in geographical exile from God's literal dwelling-place in Jerusalem. But today we do not locate God in a particular building, we have no pilgrimages to recall, no altar to return to, no enemies to hide from. There is a difference between ancient, Near-Eastern, Jewish man and modern, Western, Christian man.

But these two men have much in common: first, their common humanity. The psalmist and we are members of the same human race standing before the same Creator. Feeling cut off from God, forgotten by God, forsaken by God may be a personal reality for us too.

I think it is the sharing of a common humanity with the psalmist that explains and justifies the fact that we can read the psalm as an attempt to cope with the condition of depression— and thus find new light on the psalm as well as on coping with depression. As a human being, the psalmist had a psyche like ours. We have developed new ways of describing and analysing our experiences, but this does not mean the experiences are new. So old ways of coping with depression can still be instructive. So it is with 'spiritual depression' too; thus this psalm provided the starting-point for a book discussing that experience.[9] Again, it could be put on the lips of the death-of-God theologians, if it is right to suggest that they are really trying to cope with a situation in which God *seems* to be dead, until he returns and makes himself felt again.[1] Again, just because it expresses the typical sufferings of man, this psalm can be echoed by Jesus himself. On Palm Sunday: 'Now my soul is in turmoil, and what am I to say?' (Jn. 12:27, NEB); Jesus converses with himself, in a way reminiscent of the psalm. In Gethsemane: 'My heart is ready to break with grief' (Mt. 26:37, NEB). On the cross, he is asked mockingly, 'Where is your God?' (*cf.* Mt. 27:43). So, as we use the psalm, we can link our sufferings to Christ's; we can lay hold on the resources that he both tapped and later made available to us.[2]

[9] D. M. Lloyd-Jones, *Spiritual Depression: Its Causes and Cure* (Pickering and Inglis, 1965).

[1] *Cf.* A. Kee, *The Way of Transcendence* (Penguin Books, 1971), especially pp. 99–109 on the theme of 'waiting' (for 'God' to be real again).

[2] *Cf.* Eaton, p. 120.

So we may identify with the psalmist because we are fellow human beings who have dealings with the same God. Of course there are differences in the outward form of that relationship. Believers under the old covenant knew the real presence of God in the temple. But now Christ makes himself known wherever believers gather in his name (Mt. 18:20). You, the Christian community, says Paul, are the Holy Spirit's temple (1 Cor. 3:16). It is this gathering of believers which will be the individual believer's delight, the place of his meeting God and of his being addressed by God. The existence of this community will be an encouragement to him, even when he is cut off in one way or another from its concerns. For instance, believers sometimes find that 'the life has gone out of their prayers. To hear the words of the Collect "we to whom Thou hast given a hearty desire to pray" is disturbing and mystifying. That is exactly, as far as they can see, what God has not given them. But the words of the Collect provoke different thoughts if we ask who is the "we" to whom God is supposed to have given a hearty desire to pray . . . If we pray at all, it is because we have been brought into a praying community. And if we do not pray at all we are, if we are members of the Church, still part of a community that prays.'[3]

This living temple is a reality that more than makes up for the destruction of the material temple. It is a persisting reality because its existence is based on the achievement of one who, in his life in the world, incarnated the presence of God that was known in the temple. He could thus speak of his own physical person as the temple (Jn. 2:21), and regard discussion over whether the true temple building was to be located on this mountain or on that as redundant now that he had come (Jn. 4:21). The fullness of the Godhead dwelt in him (Col. 1:19). He is the fountain of living water (Jn. 4:10–14; 7:37–39). The plea for God to send out his light and his faithfulness to bring us to him has been answered through the one who was the light, who was full of grace and truth, who brought *God* to *us* (Jn. 1:9–18). The exodus and the covenant that the psalmist recalled have been superseded. The final sacrifice has been offered, the ultimate high priest has been granted access to the holy of holies in heaven, and all

[3] J. N. Ward, *The Use of Praying* (Epworth Press, reprinted 1973), p. 13. Kraus emphasizes the psalm's corporate significance for Christians, over against Bultmann's individualism.

those whom he represents may enter the sanctuary too (Heb. 9–10).

Christ has come, and the lament is answered. But this does not mean we can abandon the psalm. We still await a final fulfilment. There is still a dwelling-place of God in heaven to which we look forward (Rev. 21:3), a fountain of life that we are still to drink of there (21:6). Only then will the waves and the breakers of the sea be finally stilled (21:1). Only then will tears and distress be finally eliminated (21:4). Only then will the cry for vindication uttered by the elect be finally answered, and laments cease (Rev. 6:9–11; Lk. 18:1–8). Only then will worthy worship be offered to God (Rev. 4–5).

> But when I see Thee as Thou art,
> I'll praise Thee as I ought.[4]

The psalm keeps its place on our lips for a second reason—though this may be only another way of making the same point. We have noted that the believer under the new covenant enjoys fuller privileges than he did under the old. And yet it must be granted that the actual experience of spiritual realities that we enjoy often seems shallower than that to which the psalms, for instance, testify. We are in no position to take a superior attitude to Old Testament piety if we do not even find in God 'the joy of our delight' as the psalmist did in his less-privileged state. Even at best, we are ourselves in part BC men.[5] We do not live totally AD. Although Christ has come, we experience times when God seems absent, forgetful, abandoning, dead. At such times, even as Christians we may pour out our despair to God, as long as we go on to recall the objective realities of the faith, to recall our personal and corporate experience of God's love and praise and prayer, and to plead with God for a new experience of Christ in *his* grace and truth coming out to fetch us and to lead us home to God's own presence. Then, in faith in the answering of this prayer, we may wait for God, and live in praise.

[4] John Newton, 'How sweet the name of Jesus sounds'.
[5] *Cf.* John Bright, *The Authority of the Old Testament* (SCM Press, 1967), pp. 206–209, for this motif.

God help us
(Psalm 44)

The choirmaster's.   The Korahites'.   A poem.

1 *O God, we have heard with our own ears,*
  Our fathers have told us the story
  Of how you acted in their time,
  You personally in those early days.
2 *You dispossessed the nations and planted them,*
  You afflicted the peoples and let them spread out.
3 *For it was not by their own sword that they gained possession of the*
      land;
  It was not their own arm that met their need.
  It was your right hand, your arm,
  The light of your countenance, because you favoured them.

4 *You are indeed my King, O God.*
  Send help to Jacob in his need.
5 *By your power we will beat our enemies;*
  Calling on your name, we will put down our attackers.
6 *For it is not on my bow that I shall rely,*
  It will not be my sword that saves me.
7 *You saved us from our foes,*
  You humiliated those who were against us.
8 *In God we have gloried continually;*
  We will always praise your name.   *Pause*

9 *But you have abandoned us and humiliated us.*
You no longer march with our armies.

10 *You make us retreat from the enemy,*
Our foes plunder us at will.

11 *You have handed us over to be butchered like sheep,*
You have scattered us among the nations.

12 *You sell your people for next to nothing—*
You make no profit from the sale.

13 *You bring on us the scorn of our neighbours,*
The contempt and mockery of those around us.

14 *You make us a byword among the nations,*
Something for the peoples to shake their heads at.

15 *I am continually aware of my disgrace,*
My face is covered with shame,

16 *At the words of scorn and abuse,*
At the looks of the enemy taking his revenge.

17 *All this has come upon us, but we have not forgotten you,*
Nor been false to your covenant.

18 *We have not gone back on our purpose.*
Our steps have not turned from the way of life that you require.

19 *Yet you have crushed us into the place of jackals,*
Covered us with deathly darkness.

20 *If we had neglected worshipping our God*
And spread our hands in prayer to an alien god,

21 *Would not God find this out?*
He knows men's secret thoughts.

22 *On the contrary, because of you there are deaths among us continually.*
We are regarded as sheep for slaughter.

23 *Stir yourself! Why are you sleeping, Lord?*
Wake up, do not abandon us for ever.

24 *Why do you hide your face*
And put our wretchedness and our oppression out of mind?

25 *We sink down to the dust*
And lie prone on the earth:

26 *Get up and help us!*
Redeem us, to keep your own commitment to us!

Many phrases in Psalm 44 remind us of Psalms 42–43. *You have abandoned us* (9; *cf.* 43:2). *You bring on us the scorn of our neighbours* (13; *cf.* 42:10). *You have crushed us* (19; *cf.* 42:10; 43:2). We are afflicted *continually* (15, 22; *cf.* 42:3, 10). *Why do you hide your face and put our wretchedness and our oppression out of mind?* (24; *cf.* 42:2, 9). *We sink down to the dust* (25; *cf.* 42:5, 11; 43:5). Both these psalms are laments[1] and they express their distress in similar terms. But there is a difference between them, even where the verbal parallels are most marked. Whereas in Psalms 42–43 the psalmist speaks as 'I', Psalm 44 is dominated by 'we', 'us', 'our'. 'I', 'my' does come (4, 6, 15), but it is interwoven with the plural pronouns. This suggests that the 'I' is not a private individual but the congregation's representative, perhaps the king himself. Psalm 44 is sung by, or on behalf of, the people of God together.[2] And thus, whereas psalms such as 42–43 find their natural use today as expressions of the individual's sufferings and prayers (whether in corporate worship or in private prayer), community laments such as Psalm 44 will be the vehicles of the church's prayer in affliction. A prayer of the church when God seems asleep (*cf.* verse 23).

My wife and I once went to a series of seminars on personal growth and counselling. During these we were taken on imaginary journeys back into childhood and infancy. I had to try to relive being caught stealing from the till in my mother's shop when I was nine, to relive my first day at infant school, and then to try to re-experience being born, and before that living in the womb.[3] The little boy and the baby seem to be separated by a vast gulf from the parson of the same name. But there is, in fact, a historical continuity between the two; and understanding the man now involves understanding the boy then.

Understanding the Bible is a bit like one of these imaginary journeys. We have to get inside the skin of someone who lived a long time ago, whose circumstances were different, who may

[1] See above, pp. 17 ff.

[2] Pss. 60:9; 74:12; 89:50 further illustrate the 'I' interwoven with plurals. As we have noted in discussing Pss. 42–43, some interpreters regard that, too, as a congregational, or royal, psalm. Even if this is so, however, it is personal feelings that are expressed there; Ps. 44 has a more corporate and national air. Possibly the 'I' implies each member of the congregation who sings, as in hymns such as 'And can it be that I should gain . . .', 'Just as I am . . .'.

[3] LSD used to be made available to help you do that, but fortunately we were too late to have the benefit of this!

himself seem alien and difficult to understand. But he has to be understood, in his own right, if we are then to see how his experience casts light on our admittedly different circumstances—we who are in historical and spiritual continuity with him. So, as for an imaginary journey, we have to settle back and shut out the contemporary world and our personal present concerns for a time,[4] so as to open ourselves to a different world and a different set of concerns.

We are now not the church of the 1970s; we are not the growing church of the period of European missionary expansion or the vibrant, newly-alive church of the Reformation; we are not the powerful institution of the middle ages or the anxious creed-makers of the patristic period; we are not the congregation under persecution at Rome or the band of disciples at Jerusalem just commissioned to evangelize the world; we are not the little post-exilic community devoted to worship or the chastened remnant of exiles in Babylon. We are the little nation of Judah sometime before the exile. We are not a very impressive body, inwardly or outwardly; but we are the people of God, the chosen people of the Lord of heaven and earth. It is a huge claim that would not be taken seriously for a moment were it not for the fact that (to slip out of the imaginary journey for a moment) it has been vindicated by subsequent history. So we are the people of God; but at the same time we are a political entity, a nation involved in the affairs of international life of the first millennium BC. More often than not we find ourselves unable to maintain political independence, but, whether we can do this or not, we have to live in secular history, and yet at the same time to live as God's chosen people. It is a different calling from that of the church in the 1970s, and it needs to be understood in its own terms.

We are in one of those periods in our history when things have gone wrong. The occasion is the kind depicted in 2 Kings 18–19. There King Hezekiah, who from the beginning of his reign had led the nation in trust and obedience before God, and had completed a thoroughgoing reform of the syncretistic worship of Judah, is attacked by Sennacherib, king of Assyria. The Assyrians

[4] In the seminars we were told to close our eyes, to facilitate this—a dangerous invitation; I did myself fall asleep once and missed from when I was six to when I was eight, which is presumably of deep Freudian significance!

besiege Jerusalem and urge the people not to rely on the power of either Hezekiah or Yahweh to deliver them; they point to their own track-record to substantiate their claim that nothing is to be gained by resistance. Distraught, Hezekiah sends his ministers of state to consult the prophet Isaiah, and makes his own way to Yahweh's house.

It is impossible to know whether the psalm was actually used on this occasion, but it belongs to a time such as this. Military reversal leads to fervent petition. A foreign people has humiliated us, a fast has been called, we are all assembled before Yahweh in his temple in Jerusalem, and this is our prayer. It has five sections.

1. Past recollection (verses 1-3)

The psalm begins by looking back. How is it that we have this hold, albeit precarious, on a strip of land in Palestine at all? We are clear what was not the cause of it. It was not simply because of the legendary Israeli military prowess; and that is just as well. If that were the case, it would mean that everything depended now on finding another Joshua, and we might not be able to do so. But it does not depend on that.

> It was not by their own sword that [our fathers] gained possession of the land;
> It was not their own arm that met their need[5] (3).

It was not that, it was *you*, Lord. To begin with, it was the fact that *you favoured*[6] *them* (3d). The Israelites were God's favourites —that was how it all started. They found that God accepted them, that they were on the receiving end of his blessing. For reasons that only he knew, he was totally committed to them. It was not that they had earned his unexpected acceptance. 'It was

---

[5] EVV 'save', 'give victory'. The word (*yāšaʿ*) suggests deliverance in crisis— cf. PBV 'helped'. It recurs in 4, 6 and 7, and clearly constitutes an important theme in these opening sections of the psalm. On the word, see further on 42:5 above, p. 43, footnote 4.

[6] *rāṣāh*, a verb often used of God, for instance in his attitude to men and their sacrifices: he does indeed 'accept' them (Ezk. 20:40-41; Pss. 19:14; 51:16). Unconditional acceptance, acceptance of people as they are, has become an important notion today; indeed, the words are jargon. But they do express a fundamental truth about God's attitude to man.

not because you were more in number than any other people that the Lord set his love upon you and chose you, for you were the fewest of all peoples; but it is because the Lord loves you . . .' (Dt. 7:7–8, RSV). Why did the Lord love you? Because he loved you! It is impossible to suggest reasons beyond that.[7]

It is possible to see the consequences, however. God's favour was expressed in *the light of your countenance* (3d), which Aaron's blessing spoke of (Nu. 6:25–26) and the previous psalm pleaded for (Pss. 42:2, 5; 43:3).[8] Israel had God's face as her guiding light. And this in turn has practical fruit in the activity of *your right hand, your arm* (in other words, your strength[9]). These—not her own ability—are Israel's military resources. Of course the psalmist knew that on many occasions the fathers really did fight. But he regards Yahweh's aid as the crucial factor. 'History assumes a different aspect when seen by faith; it is not the vic-

[7] To try to do so, in fact, is hazardous. It easily leads to the conclusion that God's love for us is dependent on what we are or what we do; is dependent, in fact, on us. *Cf.* Snaith, pp. 61–65. The doctrine of election safeguards the principle that our salvation, our metaphysical standing, is not dependent on us, with our disastrous limitations. Two other considerations may help an understanding of this scandalous doctrine. One is that its origin lies at least partly in how salvation was actually experienced by believers in biblical times, and how it has been experienced since. Generally men do not find that they have saved themselves, but that they have been saved. They have not so much done something as had something happen to them. This was clearly the case with the Israelites' redemption from Egypt, to which the quotation from Deuteronomy above refers. They found themselves saved, and they saw others who were not. Talk of God's favour and choice gave expression to that experience. The other consideration links to this one. Israel was redeemed from Egypt not because she was more impressive than other nations and deserved to be distinguished from them, but because she was no better than other nations; but God determined to start somewhere. His purpose in the election of one is to reach the many. The election and the privilege are real; but so is the responsibility (*cf.* Rom. 11).

[8] See the comments above. Pr. 16:15 speaks of the link between the light in a human face and a man's favour; the psalm applies the idea to God.

[9] A man's right hand is usually his effective one (Pss. 45:4; 137:5). So it is, metaphorically, with God: at exodus and Sinai (Ex. 15:6, 12; Dt. 33:2), to which Ps. 44:3 looks back; in the punishment of exile and the promise of restoration (Is. 41:10; La. 2:3–4) and in any situation of need and deliverance (often in the psalms—*e.g.* 17:7; 18:35). Similarly, a man's arm stands for his strength (a mighty man is a 'man of arm' in Job 22:8): for agriculture (Is. 17:5), for shepherding (Is. 40:11), or for war (Gn. 49:24). Thus when Yahweh acts he rolls up his sleeves (Is. 52:10) and extends his arm (Ex. 6:6 and often).

tories achieved by force of arms or the heroic deeds of warriors crowned with glory, such as the heroic epic would extol, which form the subject-matter of the hymn in public worship; they are completely overshadowed by the acts of God.'[1] The same is true of the exodus and conquest narrative itself. Israel's most important contributions were to watch and to be in the right place at the right time (Ex. 14), to play musical instruments (Jos. 6), and to devise silly tricks (Jos. 8). The occasional inexplicable defeat makes the same point negatively: even when God's people are outwardly strong, what counts is whether Yahweh is involved in the action (Jos. 7). Granted this, the mere presence of the Canaanites, the Hittites, the Hivites, the Perizzites, the Girgashites, the Amorites and the Jebusites (Jos. 3:10) could not hinder the early Israelites.

> *You acted in their time,*
> *You personally[2] in those early days.*
> *You dispossessed the nations and planted[3] them,*
> *You afflicted the peoples and let them spread out[4] (1–2).*

In the place of these peoples under God's judgment, Israel was planted like a tree whose roots spread far, deep and wide in the land flowing with milk and honey.

It was important that the branches which were to grow from that tree as years went by should appreciate where they had come

[1] Weiser, on Ps. 44:1–3.

[2] Literally 'you with your hand'—the phrase emphasizes Yahweh's own instrumentality. MT links the phrase (which actually comes after 'in those early days') with the next line, but the metre is more natural with this repunctuation. NEB and Dahood may be right in going on to repoint the word for 'you' to turn it into a verb.

[3] The idea of God planting Israel goes back to the exodus story (Ex. 15:17). It recurs in connection with the growth of a tree in Ps. 80:8, which develops the picture of Israel as God's vine, once nurtured by him, but now inexplicably neglected. In their day, the prophets see ill-treatment as all it deserves, because it has failed to fruit (Is. 5; Je. 2:21; Ezk. 15). But they look forward to there being new growth, despite the stock's dead appearance (Is. 4:2; 11:1; Je. 23:5). Jesus takes up the theme (Mk. 12) and claims to be the true vine himself (Jn. 15) (both these chapters need to be understood in the light of the OT passages). See Knight, § 15.1.

[4] Like 'planting', the idea of 'spreading out' appears in Ps. 80 (verse 12) in the picture of the spreading vine, and this reinforces the implication that the picture of Israel as the vine is in mind.

from. The fact that *God* gave the Israelites the land would be a continuing stimulus to their trust, even when situations seemed hopeless (*cf.* the words of comfort in Is. 51:1–3). It would be a stimulus to maintaining the right attitudes to the one who gave it, if they were to keep hold of the land and experience his blessing there. They could be displaced in their turn, after all.

So the story of how the land came to belong to Israel had to be passed on in corporate worship and in the family circle.[5] And, say the present generation, it has been. *We have heard with our own ears, our fathers have told us the story* (1). 'I freely admit,' Calvin comments, 'that the more we think of the benefits which God has bestowed upon others, the greater is the grief which we experience when he does not relieve us in our adversities. But faith directs us to another conclusion, namely, that we should assuredly believe that we shall also in due time experience some relief, since God continues unchangeably the same.'[6]

2. *Present trust* (verses 4–8)

Lest there should be any doubt, the next paragraph in the psalm makes it explicit that the new generation does make the right response to the facts of history. It has learnt the lesson. It acknowledges that God's activity is still the key factor in Israel's story.

At the exodus Yahweh became Israel's King and began to reign over her (Ex. 15:18). At Sinai she accepted his kingship over her life (*cf.* Dt. 33:5). Here he is acknowledged afresh: *You are indeed my King, O God.*[7] If 'my' refers to the human king, who

---

[5] *Cf.* such prescriptions as Dt. 6:20–25; 31:10–13 (the nearest the OT gets to actual reference to a covenant renewal festival); Ps. 78 (see verses 3–4, leading into the narration itself). It is worth noting that the distinction between corporate worship and the family circle was not the same for the Israelites as it is for us. They were obliged to go to church, as it were, only at Christmas, Easter and Whitsun (but then for several days on end!). Unless they went to the 'high places', the worship of the family (which, no doubt, was a larger unit than the western 'nuclear family') was the basis of their week-by-week corporate life with God. To some extent one sees this pattern still among Jews, with the importance of the family's sabbath observance, though of course the development of the synagogue added a further factor to the picture. Our pattern with its near-exclusive stress on weekly church worship is culture-relative and we may have things to learn from other patterns.

[6] From his comments on 44:2.

[7] EVV redivide and repoint the middle words of verse 4, following the ancient versions. The emendation is attractive because it removes the impera-

now speaks,[8] the confession is the more significant. The monarchy was a human resort to meet a national need for effective leadership. It always formed a potential, and often an actual, infringement of Yahweh's kingship.[9] But here the king gives his own testimony that he stands under this higher authority. And on the basis of the power and favour that Yahweh has manifested in his acts on Israel's behalf in the past (1–3), the king appeals to Yahweh now: *Send help to Jacob in his need.*[1] 'The members of the Yahweh community know themselves sustained by the marvellous power of their God, at the root of which is the incomprehensible miracle of his love . . . This sure knowledge is . . . the basis for the hope of victory.'[2]

The verses that follow develop the declaration of trust made by king and people standing in the tradition of their fathers. 'We really believe what the stories and the hymns speak of. We have the same faith in Yahweh alone.' *By your power we will beat our enemies; calling on your name, we will put down*[3] *our attackers* (5). The verbs by which Israel describes the havoc she is confident of wreaking among her foes are ones used of a butting and kicking animal. Israel was happy, indeed proud, to see herself as a wild ox or a lion pouncing; but she is both by God's doing (as Balaam acknowledged: Nu. 23:21–24). *It is not on my bow that I shall rely, it will not be my sword that saves me. You saved us from our foes, you humiliated those who were against*[4] *us* (6–7). The speakers do no more than make their own what had earlier (3) been said of their

salvation

---

tive from 4 b; 4–8 is otherwise entirely a statement of trust, and prayer does not become explicit until 23–26. But MT is quite intelligible, and we cannot be sure that the psalmist was so tidy in his praying.

[8] See the introduction to this psalm, above, p. 50.

[9] See below, on Pss. 45 and 47.

[1] More literally 'command (*cf.* 42:8) the salvation (*cf.* 3 and the comments on that verse) of Jacob'.

[2] Weiser, p. 356.

[3] The verbs translated 'beat' and 'put down' are used literally of oxen ('gore', 'trample'). They are in the imperfect tense, and are capable of various translations (*cf.* JB, NEB, RSV; see on 42:8, above, p. 39). What the tense makes clear is the still unexhausted potential of the power of Yahweh. (The verbs in 7–8a are perfect.)

[4] *Those who hate* (RSV) implies that *śānē'* must refer to their feelings. But 'love' and 'hate' in the Bible indicate at least as much outward commitment (for or against) as inner feelings. This applies, *e.g.*, to Dt. 6:5; Am. 5:14–15; Mt. 6:24; I Jn. 3:18.

fathers. They have themselves proved that this is how the faith works.

An occasion described in 2 Chronicles 20 illustrates how in their history God's people experienced the reality of these truths for themselves. On that occasion, intelligence was received in Jerusalem that a joint army from the peoples the other side of the Jordan was gathering on the border. They were, in fact, already across the Dead Sea at the border oasis of En-gedi. The reaction of the leadership in Jerusalem was to call a national day of prayer, at which they sought the help of the all-powerful God, pointing out their own numerical inferiority before the invading hordes and noting the injustice of their enemies' response to their own attempts to live in peace.

The Lord's answer comes in the word of a Levite, who is given the message that the battle is in God's hands. They will not even have to fight; they will stand and watch Yahweh win the victory. And in the event, the enemies inexplicably destroy each other.

The Israelites knew such experiences, as their first forefathers did. And they had made their forefathers' response of worship their own too. *In God we have gloried continually; we will always praise your name* (8). We will pass on the testimony that we received. We will live the life of praise, as our fathers did.

Lament and praise

We may pause a moment to note that, although this psalm is designated a lament, there has so far been no explicit lamenting. Verses 1–8 could stand on their own as a hymn of praise, and in fact these verses are prescribed to be used in this way in the Church of England's 'Alternative Table of Psalms' (1971). But it is essential to their meaning to read them as the contrasting introduction to the verses that follow. The point about them is that the people's recent experience sets a question-mark against them; it is so different from that to which they formerly gave their testimony (4–8). It is possible for lament to give way to praise, as faith looks beyond distress to God's answer.[5] But sometimes praise has to give way to lament, as the following section of Psalm 44 shows (*cf.* Ps. 9). Not only is the life of the man of God passed in an alternation of prayer and praise, as he is at one time in need, at another time rejoicing in deliverance. Even within the

[5] See on 42 : 5, above, pp. 42 f.

same psalm there is this dialectic, an interplay of praise and petition. There is a dynamic cycle of lament and prayer, thanksgiving
and worship, all of whose features may appear in the same psalm.
It is a circle that may be joined and left at different points. But a
balanced life with God will manifest all these features, and our
own life with God may be tested by the psalms' pattern.

Psalm 44 illustrates three ways in which the lament or prayer of
the people of God may be related to its praise. First, its supplica-
tion makes reference to God's saving deeds *in the past*. The form
of the opening verses of the psalm (1–3), in fact, is that of a psalm
of praise; though, as we have noted, the function of these verses
is to move God to intervene because of the contrast between what
he is praised for doing in the past and what he is doing now. The
psalm goes on to a confession of trust *in the present*. Again the
outward form of the words is that of praise; now their function
is to testify to the people's continuing reliance on the God who
is praised. The note of trust is perhaps expressed also in the word
with which the psalm as a whole ends: it is a reference to God's
faithfulness, on which the psalmist still relies, and for which he
praises God. 'In the confession of trust the lament of the people
is open toward praise.' [6] The confession of trust gives way to the
commitment to praise *in the future*. The looking beyond mere
lament and petition to praise, which characterizes these psalms of
lament, is customarily expressed in the 'individual laments' in a
'vow of praise'. The psalmist promises to come back to give God
the glory when his prayer has been answered. In Psalm 44, the
people as a whole make this commitment: they have praised God
in the past, and will praise him in the future (8).[7]

3. Recent experience (verses 9–16)

After recollection, of what God has done, and present trust, in
what God is to us now, comes one of the big 'but's of the Bible
(9). Often 'but' marks the transition from bad news to good—
from lament to praise.[8] Here, however, it is the reverse. Past

---

[6] Westermann, pp. 58 f.; this section as a whole is dependent on Westermann, pp. 55–61.

[7] One of our students recently asked me if he had heard me singing to
myself 'Still praising after all these years'. It seemed an idea worth reflecting
on, and in fact a song worth singing; though I had to confess that he had mis-
heard the words of the Paul Simon song, 'Still *crazy* after all these years'!

[8] See on 49:15, below, p. 146.

recollection and present trust are in tension with what the people of God are actually experiencing now. Thus the middle third of the psalm comprises the lament section itself. If verses 1–8 stood on their own, they would make a straightforward psalm of praise; but in context, there is a pointed, almost ironic flavour to them. The Israelites know only too well the story of how God gave their fathers victory over the nations; now they are defeated and the nations gloat. They still avoid trusting in their hardware; 'nothing in their battles has changed, it seems, except the results.'[9] They have been defeated, indeed routed (9–12). They have become the objects of mockery and scorn (13–14). They in fact feel quite humiliated and demoralized (15–16).

As is often the case in the laments, the awfulness of recent experience is approached from three angles: in terms of the attitude or actions of the enemy, of the people themselves, and of God.[1]

(a) The enemy was once driven out and afflicted (2), certain to experience further devastation if he caused trouble (5), humiliated by the display of Yahweh's might (7). But now our adversaries have delivered a shattering defeat (9–12), they plunder us at will (10), and they thus have their revenge (16). Furthermore, worse (to judge from the expressions that are used) than their physical victory is the implied moral victory. They have earned the right to mockery and contempt, taunts and abuse (13, 16). They regard us as *a byword* (14a)—an object-lesson,[2] a terrible, warning example of what can happen to a people if . . . If what? The parallels suggest, 'If they disobey God' (Dt. 28:37; 1 Ki. 9:7–9; Je. 24:9; Hab. 2:6). But that is just what the people have not done (20–22 claim). Again, the enemy regard us as a sight *to shake their heads at* (14b)—not so much something amusing[3] as an object to be appalled at (*cf.* Je. 18:16). Indeed they have every right to be appalled at us; whereas they are supposed to be acknowledging that God is with us, and finding blessing through us (Gn. 12:1–3; Zc. 8:20–23).

---

[9] Kidner, commenting on verse 6.

[1] *Cf.* Westermann, pp. 53 f., where Pss. 74, 79 and 80 are compared.

[2] *māšāl*, the word regularly translated 'proverb'.

[3] *Laughingstock* (RSV) is misleading: shaking the head suggests horror, contempt and scorn (*cf.* Ps. 22:7).

(b) Conversely, whereas we once gloried in the victories given to us by our great God and expected to drive our enemies into the sea, now we in turn are devastated. We are *butchered like sheep* [4]—animals only bred to become joints of mutton, and destined for the butcher's knife from birth—and *scattered among the nations* [5] (11). We are thus demoralized: *I am continually aware of my disgrace, (i.e.) my face is covered with shame, at the words . . .* (and) *at the looks of the enemy* (15–16).

(c) *They* have routed and humiliated us; *we* are put to shame; but there also appears the second person verb which indeed dominates the picture and plumbs the depths of their affliction. *You* yourself *have abandoned us*: Yahweh's rejection is seen behind the outward events. Your attitude towards us has changed, and your behaviour towards us has changed: *you have . . . humiliated us, you no longer march with our armies* [6] (9), as you did in David's time (2 Sa. 5:24–25), or earlier when the ark went with the people and it really did signify your active presence and your battling for your people (Nu. 10:35; contrast 1 Sa. 4:3–11). It is not even that you merely neglect us. You seem to be actively against us. *You make us retreat from the enemy . . . you have handed us over* for slaughter *. . . you have scattered us* (10–11). It defies explanation. You yourself once planted us here, it is here that we live as your chosen people, and you have even destroyed that. *You sell your people* (*cf.* Dt. 32:30), an act regarded as evil when committed by human beings (*cf.* Am. 1:6, 9). And that *for next to nothing—you make no profit from the sale* (12; *cf.* NEB): like someone clearing out old clothes for a jumble sale, not because he needs the money but because they are cluttering up his wardrobe and some fool may buy them for fivepence. Yahweh's behaviour is inexplicable: he does not even gain from it. Sold to the lowest bidder! But those he sells are as a result 'completely at the disposal of their enemies,

[4] NEB: literally 'sheep for eating'.

[5] Possibly this refers to what we call *the* exile. But transportation was a widespread practice (*cf.* the warnings in Lv. 26 and Dt. 28, and the prayer of 1 Ki. 8), and may have occurred on more occasions than we know.

[6] *ṣᵉḇā'ôṯ*. The name 'Yahweh Sabaoth', 'Lord of hosts', connects Yahweh with battle; probably the idea is that his heavenly might is fighting on Israel's behalf, as her earthly forces are on the earthly battlefield (*cf.* 2 Ki. 6:17). But now the heavenly armies no longer fight, and consequently the earthly ones are defeated.

as if they were slaves, the property of their foes'.[7] 'You are responsible, Lord, for the defeat, and for its consequences in the nations' scorn and in the people's shame.' *You bring on us the scorn . . . you make us a byword* (13–14). *You* have done it, Lord. We are committed to trusting in you, glorying in you, praising you always (4–8); you have responded by abandoning us (9). The whole meaning of their lives, the possibility of the faith they have professed, is ultimately thrown into question by their experience. Can their God be understood? Their deepest problem is the problem of God himself.[8]

The laments of the people of God

It is worth pausing for a moment to consider how the lament of Israel may be instructive for the prayer of the church.

First, it would presumably have been possible to explain the defeats Israel has experienced in military terms; we are used to giving this-worldly explanations of events, explanations which are quite valid within their own terms of reference, but which may not be total explanations. The Arabs attacked on Yom Kippur and caught Israel unawares. The problems of the church arise from economic factors and social factors and cultural factors such as the effect of the Enlightenment and the Industrial Revolution. These are true explanations, but not complete ones. If they were, then there is nothing to pray about. You cannot pray to a social factor.

But behind historical causation lies God himself. Indeed, Israel in the psalm is refreshingly simplistic: she ignores the intermediate causes and speaks only of the ultimate one. When things happen, it is because God made them happen. The sun does not get up every morning of its own accord, I believe G. K. Chesterton remarked somewhere; God tells it, 'Come on, get up there'; and it does. The Old Testament speaks in these terms. God makes babies, God makes grass grow, God makes you win battles, and lose them (Pss. 139:13; 104:14; Is. 45:7). The Old Testament speaks little about other effective powers in the universe such as Satan; it prefers to safeguard the real power of God. It does not compromise his responsibility for what comes to pass in his world.

[7] Anderson, p. 341.
[8] *Cf.* Weiser, pp. 357f.

And so, when Israel wins victories, she thanks God. But when things go wrong, she does the opposite. She treats him as responsible. If we want God to put a situation right, it must be on the basis that he has made it go wrong.[9] When the church experiences defeat or failure, it is not just because she is not good at communication. The battle is a spiritual one. We need to beware of an exclusively this-worldly, impersonal explanation of events and experience. They involve supernatural factors, and they can therefore be the subject of prayer.

Secondly, we may note what an important place lament has in the psalm. It is not the climax of it, which comes in the actual petition at the end, but it is in a sense the heart of it, and is the longest of the five sections. The prominence of this feature of lament is characteristic of these psalms which in fact take their name from it. We may compare these psalms of lament with the prayers and supplications which are the equivalent for the church. We are often hesitant just to tell God about things: about what is annoying us, what is hurting us, what is frustrating us; about people, about events, about our feelings, about what we think about him. We hesitate, perhaps, to tell God things that he obviously knows already. We do not so often hesitate to suggest to him what he needs to do about situations, though this practice is at least as odd when one thinks about it.

The prayers of the Bible characteristically spend a long time telling God about the situation which needs his attention. His people in this way get things off their chest and on to his agenda.

The story of Hezekiah and Sennacherib is worth referring to again in this connection. When Hezekiah's ministers consult Isaiah, the prophet promises that the siege will soon be lifted, and it is. But Sennacherib sends word to Hezekiah that he is not to assume that Sennacherib will not be back (2 Ki. 19:1–13). Hezekiah's reaction is to return to the Lord's house and 'spread' the letter before the Lord (14).

I love this picture, partly, I think, because I can identify with it. Most of my correspondence is straightforward: I can deal with it myself, file it and forget about it. But some letters that come to me are so puzzling, or so demanding (or even so amusing!), that I have to go and knock on the door of the vice-principal or the principal and 'spread them before' him—'Have a look at this, will

[9] *Cf.* Calvin's comments on 44:11.

you, I don't know what to do about it.' This is what Hezekiah is doing before the Lord. His prayer, too (2 Ki. 19:15–19), illustrates the point we are making about laments, and indicates that it is characteristic of prayers in the Bible: one verse to acknowledge God, one verse to ask him to listen and look, two verses to describe the situation, one verse in closing to ask him kindly to do something about it (*cf.* the prayer in Acts 4:24–30).

Thirdly, we may note how important is the note of hostility in this lament, more marked than that in Psalms 42–43, and similar in fact to Jeremiah's most bitter complaints (*cf.* Je. 20). 'God, you have let me down. You have betrayed me. You are a liar. You are a sadist.' It is a hostility which assails the enemy and assails the self, but assails most vehemently the person of God. I loathe myself. I loathe them. I loathe *you*.

Now this is a community lament and it has some kind of historical origin. But it expresses, too well for this to be a coincidence, the feelings of twentieth-century schizoid man: the Outsider, the Rebel, the Dropout, the Unclubbable; even the academic theologian! The psalm's expression of the schizoid feeling is not as complete as that of Job, but it is similar.[1] The world is against me. God is against me. I despair.

In its expression of alienation and hostility the psalm is pre-Christian, but only in the sense that most of our prayers are. It in fact provides us with a vehicle for the expression of *our* feelings of total alienation and loneliness, to the one who will listen even while we are expressing our alienation from him. We may thus tell him of *our* hatred for the world (my neighbour, my boss, my tutor, my minister, my church council, my wife, my children), for ourselves, and for God. We may express them to the one who endured such hostility from sinners against himself, and absorbed it on the cross.

The loneliness of being in this position of alienation includes an inability to express the hostility and aggression that we feel. But the psalm draws it out of us, and it gives expression to this existential aloneness even as it functions as the prayer of the people of God in a particular historical crisis.

[1] Compare, this time, Frank Lake's treatment of the schizoid personality in *Clinical Theology*, especially pp. 588 f., and the Clinical Theology Association booklet on *Schizoid Personality Reactions* ([2]1971).

4. Continuing loyalty (verses 17–22)

There was, as we have noted, an obvious explanation for Yahweh's rejection of his people. They knew the warning, built into the covenant, that defeat and humiliation and abandonment by God would be the fruit of disobedience. In the psalms of lament there is often an acknowledgment that Israel has indeed sinned (*cf.* the ones in Lamentations). Psalms that refuse such a confession instead protest the psalmist's innocence (*cf.* 7; 17; 26), and this feature forms the fourth section of Psalm 44.

All this has come upon us, but we have not forgotten you, nor been false to your covenant[2] (17). If the covenant is broken, it is not through our failure. We have kept up our side of the relationship. *We have not gone back on our purpose*[3] (18a, NEB). Our attitude has not changed, and neither has our lifestyle: *our steps have not turned from the way of life that you require*[4] (18b); *if we had neglected worshipping our God*[5] *and spread our hands in prayer*[6] *to an alien god, would not God find this out?* (20–21a; *cf.* NEB). There is a crisis, and people pray in crises. But they may pray in all sorts of directions. Some Judaeans in at least one crisis prayed to Ishtar, the queen of heaven (Je. 44:15–25). But God *knows men's secret thoughts* (21b). He would know even if we hid our unfaithfulness. He knows that in fact we have not forgotten him. We have not forgotten who he is, and how all-seeing he is.

The psalmist's position reminds us of that of K in Kafka's *The Trial*, apparently regarded as guilty, but he knows not of what.

---

[2] The Hebrew does not make it clear whether the reference here is to loyalty since the trouble began and despite it (*cf.* PBV, NEB), or to faithfulness before the trouble started (*cf.* JB, RSV, TEV). Perhaps it is wrong to make this an either-or: they have always been faithful.

[3] *Purpose* is a good translation of *lēb* here. The word is usually rendered 'heart', but that gives a misleading impression. The heart can designate the seat of the emotions (4:7), but it more often refers to the mind and its thoughts (Pss. 44:21, TEV; 45:1, TEV; 48:13a, literally 'apply your *lēb* to'; 49:3) or the will and its commitment (Pss. 45:5, NEB *courage*; 51:10, 17; 55:21; 119:2).

[4] Literally 'your way'; on this phrase, see on 51:13, below, p. 169.

[5] Literally 'forgotten our God's name'. To forget is to put out of the mind and ignore (see above, on 42:9). In this context, the mention of God's name refers to calling on that name in worship.

[6] A regular posture in prayer in the Bible is to stand or kneel with arms outstretched and hands open to God (1 Ki. 8:22, 54). It may be significant that in the Bible people do not sit to pray!

Or, as in Psalms 42–43, we are reminded of Job. He too had protested his innocence (Jb. 31). But perhaps 'if Job cries out that he is innocent in such despairing accents, it is because he himself is beginning not to believe in it; it is because his soul within him is taking the side of his friends'.[7] Perhaps Israel was beginning to doubt herself too. And quite rightly, we might feel; is not their claim that they have been totally loyal to God 'the beginning of pharisaic piety'[8]? Yet they are not necessarily claiming sinlessness, only that they have been basically committed to God's will. It would be hypocritical to confess sins they had not committed in the hope of escaping a judgment they had not deserved: this was what Job's friends were condemned for wanting him to do.

Their loyalty is real, and yet they experience the punishment due to a rebel. *You have crushed us* and turned us *into the place of jackals,*[9] and *covered us with deathly darkness*[1] (19). God is lord of the powers of evil and death, and he is *letting* them have their way with us. We are broken. It is not because of our sin: *on the con-*

---

[7] Quoted by Frank Lake, *Clinical Theology*, p. 585, from Simone Weil, *Waiting on God* (Collins Fontana, 1959), p. 80.

[8] So R. Kittel, as quoted by Kraus.

[9] Such phrases are used as poetic descriptions of a desolate place, which as such becomes the dwelling of wild animals. The punishment of a city or country for its wrongdoing involves not only the destruction of its buildings, but also the desolation of its cultivable land and the loss of its population: the whole area is abandoned and allowed to go wild again. See Is. 34:9–15; Je. 9:10–12; Zp. 2:4–15; *cf.* Pedersen, pp. 454–458. Pedersen, however, regards the desert as such as belonging to the realm of what is cursed, whereas actually desert (which, after all, begins at the Mount of Olives and cannot be so alien) is the regularly traversed pasturage of sheep and their shepherds. It is only the supernaturally devastated country ($\check{s}^e m\bar{a}m\bar{a}h$, $\underline{h}orb\bar{a}h$), of which Sodom and Gomorrah are the archetype, that is in mind.

[1] This 'deep darkness' (the phrase, or compound word, comes also in Ps. 23:4; Am. 5:8; Jb. 28:3) is literally 'the shadow of death'. D. Winton Thomas (*Journal of Semitic Studies* 7, 1962, pp. 191–200) suggests that adding 'of death' in such phrases can be a way of expressing a negative superlative (we have noted above, in connection with 43:3, that Hebrew has no regular way of expressing the superlative). Nevertheless, the origin of this way of speaking lies in the fact that death itself is *the* place of darkness (Jb. 10:21–22; 38:17; and see on Ps. 49:9, 19, below). Probably the idea of the darkness of death itself is retained here: it is death's own darkness that the psalmist feels hanging over him (so also, probably, Ps. 23:4).

trary, because of you[2] there are deaths among us[3] continually. We are regarded as sheep for slaughter (22; *cf.* verse 11). All day and every day we seem to be in death's power. Such life as we have is hardly worth the name. And it is God's fault, for it has our continuing loyalty as its background. The agony of the psalm is not that we are faithful to God and afflicted by men. It is that we are faithful to God and afflicted by God. That is a much more agonizing experience.

5. Immediate challenge (verses 23–26)

At last we come, with the psalm's last paragraph, to its actual petition. There are two basic elements to the petition in a lament, and both are represented here. Turn to us! Act for us![4]

The prayer has been a long time coming, and it is startling when it arrives. *Stir yourself! Why are you sleeping, Lord?* That is what God seemed to be doing. Not that they thought that Yahweh was a dying and rising God, like those of the nations; not that this is a taunt, like Elijah's to the prophets of Baal (1 Ki. 18:27).[5] It is a cry of bewilderment,[6] 'an astonishing, otherwise unheard of, anthropomorphism, inspired in the poet by his despair'.[7] But 'God allows the saints to plead with him in this babbling manner'.[8] The Psalms are a collection of the things that God has been happy for the saints to say to him, prayers and praises that might not every time satisfy the theologian (or the superior kind of believer), but which found acceptance with God because they expressed what was in the heart of his believing

[2] 'For your sake' (JB, TEV; *cf.* RSV) is probably an overtranslation. *ʿal* can mean 'on behalf of' after verbs such as 'fight', 'speak', 'pray', 'atone': in such contexts the action is one consciously undertaken 'for the sake of' someone else. In other passages (Ps. 69:7; Je. 15:15) the phrase refers to suffering which could be described as religious persecution, and this might also be thought of as 'for your sake'. In Ps. 44:22, however, the phrase 'because of you' probably covers what is meant, namely, not that others trouble us because we are faithful to you, but that you yourself are the cause of our troubles (*cf.* 9–14). 'The reason for man's suffering and its purpose are hidden in God' (Weiser). There is again a parallel with Job.

[3] Literally 'we are being killed'.

[4] *Cf.* Westermann, *e.g.* pp. 54, 64, 67. Community laments often also include a prayer for the punishment of the oppressors.

[5] *Cf.* the comments on 42:3, above.

[6] *Cf.* the 'why's of 42:9, and the comments on this verse, above.

[7] B. Duhm, quoted by Gunkel. Only here in the Bible is God described as sleeping.

[8] Calvin, commenting on 44:23.

people—found such acceptance, in fact, that he welcomed them into his book, and implied the recognition of the activity of his Spirit in inspiring these astonishing prayers and praises. *Wake up, do not abandon us for ever* (*cf.* verse 9), he goes on, with scarcely reduced daring. *Why do you hide your face and put our wretchedness and our oppression out of mind?* We have not neglected you (20); you have neglected us (24). *Why do you hide your face?* The hiding of the face signifies rejection (Ps. 88:14; Is. 54:8), neglect (Pss. 13:1; 22:24) and punishment (Dt. 31:17). Our fathers saw the light of your face (verse 3), and that meant being accepted by you, being in your favour. Now shame covers our face (15) as the enemy turns his face in scorn towards us (16).[9] The enemy's face scornful, my face ashamed, but worst of all God's face turned away in rejection. So the psalmist's first challenge is, 'Turn your face to us'.

The second is to act on our behalf. *We sink down to the dust and lie prone on the earth* (25, NEB): do you not pity us? Will you not *do* something? *Get up and help us!* (26a). When the ark used to set out in the wilderness, Moses would say, 'Arise, Yahweh, may your enemies be scattered' (Nu. 10:35, JB). That plea is reissued. *Redeem us.* Perhaps there is an allusion back to verse 12: you sold us, now you must buy us back.

But why should God do that? The psalmist closes with an appeal not to their need, nor to what righteousness deserves, but to God's own character, to his reliability, to his faithfulness to himself, to his covenant-faithfulness, indeed to his love.[1] *Redeem us, to keep your own commitment to us!* (26b). It looks as if you are asleep, or do not care, or have forgotten us, or rejected us. But we do not believe that. 'Yahweh does not slumber or sleep' (Ps. 121:4). We believe that you are alive and that you do care about us. But you *seem* to be asleep. And when you are lethargic in this way, what arouses you is the appeal to your love. This appeal is our last word.

There is no detailing of what God is to do, only an appeal to turn and act in love. As we have noted, this is reminiscent of the prayer of Hezekiah (2 Ki. 19). Perhaps the story of Hezekiah hints at why biblical prayers are so unspecific in their actual re-

---

[9] The word *pānîm* comes each time, though this is not always clear in EVV. On the 'face' see the comments on 42:2, 5 and 11, above.

[1] These phrases attempt to express something of the flavour of *ḥesed*, on which see further, on 51:1, below.

quests: the divine response is characteristically to promise and to achieve something that no-one could have dreamed of (2 Ki. 19:20–37). How unfortunate to limit what we receive by suggesting what it might be!

Psalm 44 on the lips of the people of God

We must return to the present. We have listened to the psalm on the lips of the people of Judah. One can hear it on the lips of the exiles, when the scattering among the nations became an even more awful reality; and one can see God's response to it in his promises to the people in exile, and in the actual events of the return from exile. One can hear it being sung after the exile, by the people of the Chronicler's time, when the story of the invasion in the time of Jehoshaphat (2 Ch. 20), to which we have referred above, was actually written. Now there is a growing desperate longing for a breaking in of God into his people's history, from which he seems to have absented himself in the writer's day.

One can hear the psalm on the lips of the Jews of the Maccabaean period, when these longings became much more urgent under the pressure of times of persecution. There is in fact a story that Psalm 44 was regularly used by the Levites at this period of crisis, as a daily morning prayer at the time of the morning sacrifice, when they implored God to arouse himself and act.[2] And one can certainly hear it on the lips of the first Christians, for Paul indicates that they knew it (Rom. 8:36). Now the people of God is not a nation fighting political battles. Her enemies are the persecutors of the church, both human and supernatural. But none of these can separate us from God's love (Rom. 8:35–39). Here Paul sees the affliction of Christians against the background of God's love, as the psalm does in its last phrase. Victory can be experienced now, he asserts, before even affliction is relieved. We are not separated from God's love even when we *feel* alienated. Affliction's sharpness is blunted by the knowledge of God's love in Christ. It is only in Christ that this insight can come to clear expression, and yet the germ of it is present in the psalm: 'here

[2] Delitzsch (pp. 74 f.) passes on a passage from the Talmud (Sota 48a) which records John Hyrcanus's abolition of this practice when he thought the Levites were taking the words of the psalm too literally.

the sign of the cross already lies over the Old Testament people of God'[3]; and the people of God under both dispensations need to accept that the cross is a calling which it should not find surprising: 'lest, therefore, the severity of the cross should dismay us, let us always have present to our view this condition of the Church, that as we are adopted in Christ, we are appointed to the slaughter.'[4] In the situation of affliction, of the feeling that God has let his people down, the New Testament also encourages them to bid him awake out of slumber, for in the incarnation it offers them exactly the experience of the Lord sleeping and needing to be awakened to their peril (Mk. 4:38).[5]

Further, we can hear the psalm on the lips of Christians since New Testament times. Ambrose died as he reached verse 23 in a commentary on this psalm: *Stir yourself! Why are you sleeping, Lord? Wake up, do not abandon us for ever.*[6] For Calvin, the persecutors were the papists, against whom verse 20 could usefully be used as a condemnation of praying for the saints.[7] Shortly after Calvin's death the psalm was on the lips of other protestants mourning the massacre of the Eve of St Bartholomew's Day, 1572;[8] and it found its way into the Church of England's Litany, which brings the first and last verses of the psalm together, as a prayer for the church.

And we can continue to use this prayer for the church today. We too have heard from our fathers the great things of the past. Can we go on through the psalm? Can we still declare our trust in the old message, of what God has done for his people, and for the world? Are we still committed to the old method, of trust in his power and not in what might be expected to be more effective in this world (*cf.* 1 Cor. 1–2), as we do battle with the forces that work against the gospel? Do we ourselves face, and do we face God with, the feeble realities of the situation the church is often in? A bishop tells of the vicar expressing his sense of achievement at the attendance of 300 at his family service: 'But where are the other 14,700 parishioners?' the bishop asked. What about churches of much smaller numbers hiding from the truth of the

[3] Kraus, p. 329.
[4] Calvin, p. 171.
[5] *Cf.* Kidner, p. 170.
[6] So Prothero, p. 18.
[7] See Calvin's comments on the passage.
[8] *Cf.* Prothero, pp. 264 f.

insignificance of the church's place in the community, and consequently not laying it before God? What about those of us who are so concerned for the church of the future that we, too, fail to face up to the reality of the church of the present? What we do not face up to, we cannot pray about; what we do not pray about, we cannot expect to improve.

Can we ourselves claim a continuing loyalty to God? And, finally, have we actually issued the challenge to God that, by accepting this psalm into his book, God invites us to issue? Do we assume that we have to wait till the tide turns, or the sociological situation changes, or the millennium arrives, before we see God showering blessing on his people? Can we not hope to see the Lord's face shining in blessing before then? *Our fathers have told us the story of how you acted in their time*, ... Now *get up and help us! Redeem us, to keep your own commitment to us!*

If God is King
(Psalms 45 and 47)

45 *The choirmaster's. To Lilies. The Korahites'. A poem. A love-song.*

1 *My mind pours forth good tidings,*
I address my work to a king,
My tongue is like the pen of an expert scribe.
2 *You are the most handsome of men;*
Your lips are moulded in grace.
So God has given you perpetual blessing.
3 *Fasten your sword to your side, mighty warrior,*
In your splendour and your majesty,
4 *And in your majesty ride on triumphantly*
For the cause of truth, and bring justice to the weak.
You will be marked out by the awesome deeds of your right hand—
5 *Your sharpened arrows—*
Peoples are beneath your feet—
They fall in the heart of the king's enemies.
6 *The throne that God has given you will always be yours.*
Your royal sceptre rules with uprightness.
7 *You love right and hate wrong:*
So God, your God, has anointed you above your fellows
With oil, the token of joy.
8 *Myrrh, aloes and cassia fill your clothes.*
From a palace panelled with ivory strings make you glad.
9 *Princesses are adorned in your jewels.*
A queen stands at your right in gold from Ophir.

10 *Listen, daughter, consider and give heed:*
    Forget your people and your family.
11 *The king will desire you in your beauty;*
    He is your lord; bow down to him.
12 *The people of Tyre will delight you with gifts,*
    The richest of people with all wealth.
13 *The princess is within, her dress of embroidered gold;*
14 *In brocaded gown she is led to the king.*
    The bridesmaids who follow her are brought to you,
15 *They are escorted with gladness and joy,*
    They come to the king's palace.

16 *In place of your fathers you will have sons,*
    You will make them rulers throughout the world.
17 *I will cause your name to be remembered to all generations:*
    Thus peoples will acknowledge you for all time.

47   *The choirmaster's.   The Korahites'.   A psalm.*

1 *All you peoples, clap your hands!*
   Shout to God with a resounding cry!
2   *For Yahweh the Most High is to be acknowledged with awe,*
     A great King over all the world.
3   *He puts peoples under our dominion,*
     Nations beneath our feet;
4   *He chooses the land that we are to possess,*
     The pride of Jacob whom he loved.   *Pause*
5 *God has gone up to a shout,*
   Yahweh has gone up to the blast of a trumpet.

6 *Make music for our God, let it sound!*
   Make music for our King, let it sound!
7   *For God is King of all the world:*
     Sing well!
8   *God is become King over the nations,*
     God has taken his seat on his holy throne.
9   *The nobles of the peoples are gathered*
     As the people of the God of Abraham.
   The world powers belong to God,
   For he has taken himself up to the highest.

72

Psalms 45 and 47 are both about kingship.

My mind[1] pours forth good tidings, I address my work to a king, my tongue is like the pen of an expert scribe[2] (45:1).
Make music[3] for our King, let it sound! (47:6).

Peoples are beneath your feet (45:5).
He puts peoples under our dominion, nations beneath our feet (47:3).

Peoples will acknowledge you for all time (45:17).
All you peoples, clap your hands! (47:1).

The psalms refer to two different kings, however. In Psalm 47 it is God as *the King of all the world* (7). In Psalm 45 it is someone to whom *God has given blessing* (2), whom *God, your God has anointed* (7): the human king. There are two kings, two kingships. What, then, is the relationship between them? Where does authority and responsibility lie?

THE DIVINE KING (Psalm 47)

It is appropriate to look at Psalm 47 first, for the divine King is theologically prior to the earthly king. He is the King of kings. As all fatherhood receives its meaning from his fatherhood (Eph. 3:14–15), so all kingship is derived from his.[4] Historically, too, Israel had God as her King both before she had an earthly monarch (*cf.* Ex. 15:18; 1 Sa. 8:7) and after the earthly monarchy ended with the exile.

---

[1] *lēb*; see on 44:18, above, p. 64.

[2] The third clause of this opening verse is parallel to the first. His mind is bubbling (the expression comes from cooking) with things to say; he sings out of a full heart, as a scribe teaches out of a full knowledge (*cf.* Ezr. 7:6 for the final phrase). The verse as a whole suggests both his own creativity and the awareness that what is said is 'given' him. He is active, yet inspired. See further the comments on 49:3–4, below.

[3] *zāmar*, which puts the emphasis on the music: it covers both singing and playing. The word for 'psalm', *mizmôr*, comes from this root; it means a religious *song* (BDB 'melody'). *Saying* the psalms is a very strange occupation!

[4] Of course, philosophically, ideas such as fatherhood and kingship will be seen as models drawn from human experience and applied to God analogically. Thus our understanding of such ideas depends (to some extent) on our experience of the earthly realities. Nevertheless the *meaning* of the human forms is secondary: the aspects of God that we describe in terms of kingship or fatherhood belonged to God before they belonged to man—but then man was made in God's image and can therefore speak analogically of God.

Christians have used Psalm 47 on Ascension Day, and it does celebrate the 'ascension' of God the King:

> *God has gone up to a shout,*
> *Yahweh has gone up to the blast of a trumpet* (5).

The language here follows the description in 2 Samuel 6 of how David brought up Yahweh's ark to Jerusalem. The ark was a container for the slabs of stone inscribed with the ten commandments, the basic covenant (*cf.* Dt. 10:1–5). It thus stood for the covenant relationship between Yahweh and the people. At the ark, in the tabernacle, the Lord met with his people (*e.g.* Jos. 7:6). Saul took the ark into battle against the Philistines, hoping thereby to be sure of Yahweh's presence and power, but he was defeated and the ark was captured (1 Sa. 4). The Philistines found the ark too hot to handle, however, and returned it (1 Sa. 5–7). Then, when David made Jerusalem his capital, he installed the ark in a tent there: 'David and all the house of Israel brought up the ark of the Lord with shouting, and with the sound of the horn' (2 Sa. 6:15). From this time on, the ark symbolized Yahweh's lordship over Israel, exercised from Jerusalem.

Psalm 47 looks back to this occasion and expresses its conviction that Yahweh reigns now in terms derived from this story. Indeed it may well reflect a ceremony each year in which Israel celebrated Yahweh's taking up his throne on Mount Zion, as he did on that historical occasion.

The same event is referred to in the last line of the psalm:

> *The world powers belong to God,*
> *For he has taken himself up to the highest* (9).

The congregation have celebrated Yahweh's taking up his dwelling on Mount Zion, and they acknowledge his lordship exercised from there. At the same time, *God has gone up* would recall a less earthly idea, that of God going up to heaven (which the temple, as his dwelling-place in this world, symbolized). The earthly ascension is the symbol of a heavenly one. In both senses, Yahweh is the ascended, exalted God.

The realization that Yahweh is ascended lies behind the whole of Psalm 47. It has two stanzas, with parallel structure:[5]

[5] The structure is not made clear by the paragraphing in EVV.

The stanzas are parallel, and the individual components complement each other. To acclaim God means to clap and to *shout to God with a resounding cry* (1)[7]; it also means to *make music[8] for our King* (6). The ark, the symbol of Yahweh's presence and power, was being carried with ceremony into the temple. Trumpets were blowing, the crowd was cheering, the choir was singing, the band was playing. The enthusiasm and the sound were apparently more reminiscent of a Cup Final at Wembley or, more relevantly, of a coronation[9] than of the average church service!

Both stanzas ground this acclamation in the fact of Yahweh's kingship in relation to *all the world* (2, 7). He is thus to be acknowledged with awe by the nations, over whom he is king without their having realized it or having had the chance to decide whether they like the idea (2). Indeed Psalm 2 implies (and history supports the suggestion) that the world rulers would not in fact make acknowledging Yahweh their instinctive choice. They bow down before him because they face facts: he *is* the real King over the world which they claim to rule. He is *a great King*: perhaps there is an allusion to the Assyrian emperor's claim to this title as no mere king but a king among kings. Alternatively (or in addition) the psalm contradicts the claim of Baal to be king. It is really Yahweh to whom this honour belongs.[1] He is *the Most*

[6] Verses 2 and 7 begin *kî*, 'for', but most EVV omit.

[7] There is no reference to music or singing in verse 1; it refers to the sound of clapping and shouting. The word usually translated 'of joy' (*rinnāh*) refers to a 'ringing cry' (BDB) which can express distress or exhortation as well as joy: it is the *sound* which is referred to, not the motive. The realization that verse 1 refers to acclamation, which does not necessarily imply rejoicing, eases the development into verse 2, with its reference to fear. The believer does of course feel both fear and joy before God, but usually one or other is dominant at any given moment!

[8] See the comments on verse 6, above, p. 73.

[9] *Cf.* 2 Ki. 11:12; and see the comments on 47:8, below, pp. 78 ff.

[1] See, further, the comments on 48:2, below, pp. 113 ff.

High, '*Elyon*'. El Elyon first appears in the Bible as the God of Melchizedek, the priest-king of Jerusalem; Abraham identifies El Elyon with his own God, Yahweh (Gn. 14:18–22). El appears subsequently in Genesis as El Roi, the God who sees (16:13), El Shaddai, the Almighty God (though the background of this title is uncertain) (17:1), El Olam, the Everlasting God (21:33), and so on, and these are understood as different ways of speaking of *the* mighty God (who was also the mightiest god for the Canaanites). Possibly these different titles were associated with different places of worship: if El was worshipped as Elyon especially at Jerusalem, this would explain the prominence of this title in the psalms, which come from the time when Jerusalem had become an Israelite city. From Jerusalem the world is ruled by *Yahweh* (the God who particularly revealed himself to the Israelites, involved himself in their history, and looked after them in their need) *El* (the mighty creator, acknowledged even by the Canaanites to be the king even of the other so-called gods) *Elyon* (the Most High, the exalted, ascended one): the threefold title *Yahweh El Elyon* actually occurs in Psalm 50:1. This mighty God is the *great King over all the world*, who as such indeed *is to be acknowledged with awe*—the word denotes 'that quality of God which inspires fear and terror in his enemies . . . but worshipful awe and a spirit of praise in the righteous'.[2]

The parallel line in the second stanza (7) takes up the theme of acclaiming God's kingship and adds a new role. Yahweh has already been described as *our King* (6), and as King he is acknowledged not only with reverence but with music. *God is King of all the world: sing well*.[3] The challenge is issued now not to the nations, but to the people that calls Yahweh 'our King' and rejoices to make music to him.

But how is it known and manifested that Yahweh is King? Both stanzas assert that this lordship is evidenced in history. His reign is no mere constitutional monarchy, but one with real power.

[2] Anderson, p. 468.
[3] More literally, 'make music with (a) *maśkîl*'. The latter word comes in the psalm headings (*e.g.* 42, 44, 45), where it seems to be a type of composition. But here most EVV take it adverbially (the root *ś-k-l* has a range of meanings including 'skill', 'insight' and 'contemplation'). We can at least be sure that it is a *good* type of singing!

He puts peoples under our dominion,
Nations beneath our feet;
He chooses the land that we are to possess,
The pride of Jacob whom he loved (3–4).

For a significant, though limited, period of her life, from Moses
to the exile, God's people was a nation like other nations. She was
involved in history, in politics, in war. God's presence with her
thus took him into these areas: it was here that he revealed his
power and his purpose. He proves he is God by the victories he
gives to his people. But they are righteous victories. The Canaanites lose their land because of their wickedness (Lv. 18:24–25;
Dt. 9:4–5), which Israel is Yahweh's means of punishing.

But the psalmist's mind at this point is not occupied with the
righteousness of these victories. He thinks first of the simple fact
of them—of the power of Yahweh, of the amazing fact that
nations submit to little Israel. This leads the psalmist to express
his awareness of the grace of God shown in these events (4):
election and love toward Israel are involved in them, as well as
righteousness toward the nations. God indeed allocated the lands
that all the nations were to possess (Dt. 32:8).[4] But this statement, with all its implied assertion of the universality of God's
reign and his caring for all peoples—all are his possession (Ps.
82:8)—is immediately followed by a declaration of the special-
ness of Jacob: *he* is Yahweh's possession (Dt. 32:9).[5] *He chooses*
the land that we are to possess[6] (*cf.* Dt. 4:21). The land itself, too,
can be spoken of as Yahweh's (Je. 2:7); it is by implication, then,
something special, a land flowing with milk and honey (*e.g.* Dt.
6:3), comparing so favourably with the Israelites' lot in Egypt or
their wanderings in the wilderness. Thus it is the object of the
rightful *pride of Jacob*, the evidence that Jacob was the one *whom*

[4] It may be significant that God is called Elyon (Most High) in Dt. 32:8.
[5] Again, note the reference to Jacob here, as in Ps. 47:4.
[6] 'He chooses our inheritance' (EVV)—the word *naḥªlāh* refers to a personal
possession, generally received as a gift from someone else; it need not necessarily refer to a handing over from father to son. It does suggest sure
possession, under God. On the other hand, it is possible that 'our *naḥªlāh*'
refers not to the land (which is not elsewhere spoken of as 'chosen' by
Yahweh) but to the hill of Zion, Yahweh's dwelling (*cf.* Ps. 132:13). It, too,
is Yahweh's 'possession' (Ex. 15:17); the temple is Israel's 'pride' (Ezk.
24:21). The point would be a natural one to make when worshipping *in* the
temple on Mount Zion.

he loved (*cf.* Dt. 4:37–38). It is his continuing gift to them. Their enemies will try to deprive them of this *possession* (*e.g.* 2 Ch. 20:11), but so long as they are obedient they will carry on being victorious.

The emphasis in these statements about God's activity in history (3–4) is that they are not yet completed. But how does Israel know Yahweh is at work? Sometimes experience seems to belie it. She is defeated rather than triumphant. Her possession of the land can be questioned. Whence come her confident affirmations that Yahweh's work will be completed, that it *is* going on? The parallel statements in the second stanza emphasize that it *has* begun; and this is the basis for hope in the present and for the future. God has begun to reign.[7]

> God is become King[8] *over the nations,*
> *God has taken his seat on his holy throne.*
> *The nobles of the peoples are gathered*
> *As the people of the God of Abraham* (8–9a).

'God has begun to reign.' This statement could be misunderstood. When the same phrase is used at an earthly king's accession (2 Ki. 9:13), the situation presupposes that until this moment the particular person was not reigning. Clearly we do not imply this when we use parallel statements in our hymns: 'Ride on! Ride on in majesty! . . . Then take, O God, Thy power, and reign.' 'Christ the Lord is risen today!' In singing such words we do not imply that Jesus dies and rises again each year, but that *we* 'go through' the events again and seek to lay hold of the power in them, to make that reign real for ourselves. We may be tempted to doubt whether all authority in heaven and on earth is given to Christ (Mt. 28:18), but we remind ourselves of Easter and

[7] The point being made here depends on the fact that the verbs in 3–4 are imperfect (except the one in the subordinate clause, 4b, where the reference is, I take it, to the love God first set on Jacob in the past); all those in the corresponding two couplets in the second stanza (8–9a) are perfect. I doubt if this is chance; on the significance of perfect and imperfect, see the comments on 42:8, above, p. 39.

[8] *God reigns* (EVV) is equally possible grammatically. But the psalms that speak in this way (*cf.* 93:1; 96:10; 97:1; 99:1) seem to celebrate some specific event, rather than a general truth, and the cluster of perfect verbs makes this especially likely here.

declare that the kingdom of this world *has become* the kingdom of our Lord and of his Christ, that God *has begun* to reign (Rev. 11:15, 17).

Similarly, Israel may well have thought of Yahweh taking up his reign again each year, without this implying that in the meantime he had lost it.

The same is true with the assertion that *God has taken his seat on his holy throne*. Now God's throne is in heaven (1 Ki. 22:19; Is. 66:1), and the cherubim and seraphim are his heavenly attendants or bearers (Ps. 18:10; Is. 6:2–6; Ezk. 1; 10). But he is also spoken of as enthroned on the earthly cherubim (1 Sa. 4:4), which were put above the covering (the 'mercy-seat') over the ark in the tabernacle and temple (Ex. 37:1–9; 1 Ki. 6:19–28). It seems that the tabernacle or temple is an earthly equivalent to God's dwelling in heaven; he is enthroned in heaven, but he is also enthroned on earth. Thus, when he is spoken of as 'enthroned upon the cherubim' (Pss. 80:1; 99:1), it may be difficult to decide whether the heavenly or the earthly figures are meant. Indeed probably both are in mind, in that one represents the other.

Now the occasion when God was enthroned in Zion, when he became King there, was when his dwelling was established, first in David's tabernacle and then in Solomon's temple (2 Sa. 6; 1 Ki. 8), in Jerusalem. But, as we yearly celebrate Christmas, Easter and other festivals, so Israel yearly celebrated Passover, Tabernacles, and so on. At such a festival,[9] the events that made Yahweh King over Israel in Jerusalem were celebrated, and perhaps the ark was again carried in procession, again installed on Zion. Once more Yahweh took up his seat on his holy throne and began to reign. And once more the nobles of the peoples gathered as the people of the God of Abraham. Israel was never called to be a missionary people. She was called to be an attractive, accepting people. The nations would be so impressed by the blessing of 'the people of the God of Abraham' that they would seek the same for themselves (Gn. 12:1–3, especially NEB). From the beginning of Israel's history individuals did in fact respond to what

---

[9] Scholars usually reckon it was Tabernacles, though there is little hard evidence, and it may well have been Passover (since the first declaration of Yahweh's Kingship comes in connection with the Passover story, Ex. 12–15). On the other hand, trumpets were blown (*cf.* Ps. 47:5) at Tabernacles, for the New Year (Lv. 23:24).

they saw Yahweh had done: Jethro the Midianite priest (Ex. 18:10–12), Rahab of Jericho (Jos. 2:9–11), Naaman the Syrian general (2 Ki. 5:15, 17). Indeed whole clans or towns recognized that Yahweh's power was with Israel (Jos. 9) and agreed to abandon other gods that they might serve Yahweh alone (Jos. 24). In the high days of the monarchy, Hiram and the queen of Sheba blessed Yahweh for what he had done for Solomon (1 Ki. 5:7; 10:9), and perhaps representatives of subject peoples such as the Ammonites came to the great festivals in Jerusalem. All these events might provide evidence that the nations were joining Abraham's people in acknowledging Yahweh (*cf.* Ps. 102:21–22), and perhaps this event, too, was symbolized in the festival itself.

So Israel recalls what God has done (8–9a) and declares her faith in what he can do and is doing now (3–4). If she is tempted to doubt the present verbs of verses 3–4, she can reassure herself by the past verbs of verses 8–9a.

A further difference between these pairs of couplets appears in the description of the nations' fate. We have noted that in the second stanza they seem to be taking their place among the people of Abraham; but earlier they had been prostrate beneath this people (3). In so far as the nations are seen as in wilful rebellion against Israel's God, they are to be put down; but in so far as they are seen as in regretful ignorance of Israel's God, they are to be invited to join in his worship. One way or another, they will bow: of their own free will or under compulsion, in sullen submission or in humble worship.[1]

The 'princes of the peoples' reappear in the final line of the psalm (9). We have already glanced at this in beginning from the idea of God being 'ascended', but it is appropriate that we should return to this note of the exaltation of God, as the psalm itself ends in this way. *The world powers belong to God, for he has taken himself up to the highest.* 'He alone is the Lord who has at his disposal all the forces of war; no human power will arise any more. The idea of God's everlasting Kingdom of peace seems to

---

[1] Perhaps the relationship between these two approaches to the fate of the nations (which appear alongside each other also in Is. 40–55, *e.g.* 42:1–12; 49:22–26) is elucidated by the insight which comes to clearer expression in the New Testament, that conversion is both an acceptance of God's judgment on us, and a casting of ourselves on the God who not only condemns but also loves us.

be reflected in this statement; presumably it seeks to give expression to a thought similar to the one the prophets have in mind when they say that Yahweh makes wars cease in all the world (Isa. 2.4; 9.5; Zech. 9.10; Ps. 46.9). At the end of the psalm the thoughts are exclusively focused on God who as the only One who is highly exalted sits enthroned for ever as the Lord of the whole world.'[2]

THE HUMAN KING (Psalm 45)

Psalm 45 is a very different kind of lyric psalm, a song for a marriage. The title refers to it as a love-song. Though perhaps composed for a particular king's marriage, it was presumably used (like other psalms) on many occasions: perhaps each year at Israel's equivalent to 'the Queen's birthday', or at least at each king's wedding.

The Bible and the apocrypha describe several marriages. There is much variation in the customs that these pictures reveal, but certain features recur (and can sometimes be paralleled in the lives of Middle Eastern peoples today). A marriage is arranged not solely (if at all) at the desire of the couple, but through the negotiations of their parents; love usually comes after the marriage, not before it (cf. Gn. 24:67). The actual marriage consists fundamentally in the public receiving of the bride into the groom's house (Gn. 24:67). Naturally, it is an occasion of much festivity. The groom is evidently dressed for the occasion as he awaits the arrival of his bride, surrounded by his own family. Apparently he goes to meet her to bring her to her new home (Ps. 45:2-9; also 1 Macc. 9:37-39; Mt. 25:1-12). She in turn is adorned in her finery, a dress made of yards of the richest material, with jewels and other adornment, such as she will recall all her life (Ps. 45:9, 13-14; also Is. 61:10; Je. 2:32; Rev. 21:2). Her bridesmaids accompany her from her old home to her new one, and the whole community rejoices (Ps. 45:13-15).[3]

But what is a royal wedding-song doing in the Bible? First, love and marriage are topics the Bible treats as God's concerns;

[2] From Weiser's comments on Ps. 47:9.
[3] As well as the passages cited, see Gn. 29; 34; Jdg. 14; 1 Sa. 18:17-29; Tobit 7-11; and the Song of Songs, which is a collection of love-songs which may have their origin in wedding-songs. See further de Vaux, pp. 26-34.

indeed he invented them (Gn. 1–2). The Song of Songs offers a whole series of lyric evocations of this theme. God wants men to enjoy this gift, like all those he has given to us. God declared that marriage, like food, was something good, and something to be accepted with thanksgiving, as a gift (1 Tim. 4:3–5). God's own evaluation of marriage as a good gift of creation, combined with a prayerful acceptance of it as his gift, makes getting married a sacred occasion.

But then a king's marriage will be especially important. Anything to do with the king was of significance for the whole people, because his life so affected theirs. Their happiness, their prosperity, their righteousness, were tied up with his. So, before God, they celebrate his wedding, pray for God's blessing on him and challenge him to fulfil the royal responsibility that God has given him.

The psalm does not have a clear structure, except that the royal groom is addressed in verses 1–9 and 16–17, while verses 10–15 address the royal bride. Within these sections, however, are interwoven three elements: the compliments given to each, the challenge given to each, and the promise given to each.

The compliments

To the king: *You are the most handsome of men; your lips are moulded in grace* (2).[4] There is a hint in this passive verb that the graciousness is something given. A man has no reason to be proud of the appearance with which he is endowed, or of his natural gift for words. These are indeed gifts, from the one who created him. But, while there is thus no basis for pride in them, they can be acknowledged and rejoiced in by others. Their presence leads to the conclusion, *so*[5] *God has given you perpetual*[6] *blessing* (2c). Israel assumes that the man of God's choice will look and sound like it. Saul was handsome, tall and wealthy (1 Sa. 9:1–2). David was of fair complexion, beautiful eyes and handsome appearance (1 Sa.

---

[4] *Cf.* NEB for 2b; a more literal translation is, 'grace is poured (like oil, or like metal being used for casting) on your lips'.

[5] *ᶜal-kēn* means 'therefore', not 'because' (JB); but the argument is not 'because of these qualities God has blessed you', but 'because of these qualities we know God has blessed you' (*cf.* BDB, p. 487).

[6] *lᵉᶜōlām* (EVV *for ever*) means 'in perpetuity'; whether this is metaphysically 'for ever' or 'for life' or 'until anything happens to change the situation' depends on the context.

16:12). An interest in such qualities is not incompatible with an emphasis on what a man is inside; indeed the two are expected to reflect each other. The one major exception to this rule was thus to be a puzzle (Is. 53:1–2).

God's blessing is explicitly connected with the king's moral qualities subsequently in the psalm. *Your royal sceptre rules with uprightness. You love right and hate wrong* (6b–7a). Right and wrong were the king's business. His prestige and his privilege depended on his taking this commitment seriously (*cf.* the prominent concern for 'right' in Ps. 72's challenge to and prayer for the king).[6a] *So God,[7] your God, has anointed you above your fellows with oil* (7, NEB). A king was anointed when he took the throne, anointed by the priest in God's name. Thus he is 'the anointed one', the *meṣ̌iaḥ*. Here, however, another anointing seems to be meant, part of the wedding celebration. On this occasion, the fragrance of *myrrh, aloes and cassia* (8; *cf.* Ct. 3:6), aromatic substances which came from various trees, so permeated the king's clothing that it seemed to be made of them.[8]

The point about these substances was both their fragrance (they were used for perfume as well as for anointing oil) and what they symbolized, for oil is *the token of joy* (7, NEB). The joy was expressed in the wedding music, too: *from a palace panelled with ivory[9] strings make you glad* (8). The festivity in the home, which has been his and is about to be hers too, beckons him to bring her inside. It is a day when the royal family adorn themselves to honour him: *princesses are adorned in your jewels[1]* (9a).

The thought of these royal ladies leads to that of the one for whom the king had come. *A queen stands at your right in gold from Ophir[2]* (9b). The actual moment of marriage is embodied in this

[6a] 'Love' and 'hate' denote not merely feelings but practical commitment: they indicate taking care about or opposing; *cf.* on 44:7, above.

[7] A clear example of a verse where 'Yahweh' will have been the original version; *cf.* the comments on 42:8, above, pp. 38 f.

[8] Literally 'your clothes are myrrh and aloes, cassia'. *Cf.* GK 141d.

[9] NEB, taking the plural noun (RSV *palaces*) as referring to its various buildings. Ivory panelling suggested luxury and splendour (*cf.* Am. 3:15; 6:4).

[1] From the adjective *yāqār*, which usually means 'precious', often in the compound phrase 'precious stones'. This idea makes sense here in parallelism with *gold from Ophir* in the next line (*cf.* Anderson). The translation 'ladies of honour' etc. in EVV is difficult to parallel for this word.

[2] Where Ophir was, no-one knows; but it was evidently the best quality gold!

standing side-by-side together before their families and com-
munities. And the queen now comes into prominence in her own
right. As the psalmist had observed how handsome the groom
was, now he notes the bride's beauty (11). As he had pictured the
groom's appearance as he was about to be joined by her, so now
he imagines her about to come to her groom and king: *The princess is within, her dress of embroidered gold*[3]; *in brocaded gown she is led
to the king* (13–14a). The psalmist changes his manner of speaking and addresses the king direct: *The bridesmaids who follow her are
brought to you,*[4] *they are escorted with gladness and joy, they come to the
king's palace* (14b–15). It is a day of celebration and rejoicing
indeed.

The challenge

The psalm interweaves its compliments and word-pictures with
something more demanding, however. We have noted that the
king plays a key role in Israel's life with God and her life in the
world. He is the one through whom God's justice is put into
effect. Thus we soon move from the nice things that have to be
said at a wedding, to the challenge, 'Act as God's vicegerent'.

> *Fasten your sword to your side, mighty warrior,*
> *In your splendour and your majesty,*
> *And in your majesty ride on triumphantly*
> *For the cause of truth, and bring justice to the weak* (3–4).

The king is handsome and graceful (2); but he is not soft. As
king, he is bound to be involved in war. But the encouragement
he is given relates force to moral goals; it is not merely a means
of expansion, or even of defence, but of justice. *Splendour* and
majesty belong to God as King (Ps. 96:6), but he bestows them on
the human king (Ps. 21:5). As God shows them in his deeds (Ps.
111:3), so must the king.

The challenge to the queen comes in verses 10–11; the psalmist

---

[3] The general sense of these verses is clear, but the same is not true of how
they fit together. The translation generally follows RSV, which connects the
opening words of 13 with the preceding verse (to be commented on below).

[4] EVV follow two MSS which read *to her, lāh*, instead of *to you, lāk*. But this
looks like an attempt to simplify. Hebrew easily switches from talking *to*
someone (second person) to talking *about* him (third person), and vice versa,
and this switch is made several times in Ps. 45 with regard to the king.

speaks with a fatherlike authority, in the manner of a priest or prophet or wise man, at this solemn occasion.

> *Listen, daughter, consider and give heed:*
> *Forget your people and your family.*
> *The king will desire you in your beauty;*
> *He is your lord*[5]*; bow down to him.*

Perhaps the queen was a foreigner (*cf.* 12, NEB); kings often took brides from other nations, for diplomatic reasons, though the practice often led to trouble (*e.g.* 1 Ki. 11). If she was from another people, then telling her to forget her background has a special point. She is exhorted to become a true Israelite, like Ruth (Ru. 1:16). 'There is ... a suggestion of the Israelite temple poet's recollections of the evils ensuing for the faithful when a foreign princess like Jezebel was unwilling to forget her father's house, seeing it as her duty to introduce the cult of Baal among Yahweh's people: that must not happen again.'[6]

There is more certainly something important here about all marriage. There is a new man in the bride's life now. The marriage service brings out this point: the bride's father takes her hand for the last time and gives over the bride to her groom. The way of giving expression to this point is pre-women's lib, but the point is important. Old ties, old patterns of behaviour, old relationships are broken (in the form they have existed so far: they will have to be remade, of course, but in a new form). The new relationship takes over from the old one. Many problems in marriages are caused by the father's not giving the bride away, by the bride's not forgetting her father's house. So the challenge of marriage is to give something up: but the psalm does not stop there.

The promise

The princess has, in a sense, to forget her old family. But she is promised that the pain likely to be involved in this (for any normal daughter may experience a certain pain in turning her back on the ties that have meant so much) will be worth while.

[5] The word *'aḏôn* can mean both 'master' and 'husband', and both meanings are relevant here.

[6] Mowinckel, I, p. 73.

As she loses them, she will win him. He will *want*[7] her (11). The wedding presents will be worth while, too:

> *The people of*[8] *Tyre will delight you with gifts*
> *The richest of people*[9] *with all wealth*[1] (12).

The king, too, has to turn his back on the past. At the beginning God declared that at marriage 'a man leaves his father and his mother . . .' (Gn. 2:24); but a man, too, can fail to be detached from his past relationship with his family. He too is given a promise in this connection: *In place of your fathers you will have sons* (16). As the woman turns from her former home, so the man finds a 'new orientation to the future, to be a parent rather than a son'[2]: he is promised the fulfilment of being a proud father.

But the promises given to the king concern not only his marriage but also his rule. As the compliments included his commitment to right (7) and the challenge included the exhortation to fight for Yahweh's justice (4), so the promise includes success in this battle:

> *You will be marked out by the awesome deeds of your right hand*[3]
> *Your sharpened arrows—*
> *Peoples are beneath your feet—*
> *They*[4] *fall in the heart of the king's enemies* (4c–5).

There will be something supernatural about the victories the king wins. It is his *right hand* that fights; but the achievements have the mark of God's *awesome deeds*[5] about them. And thus they bring

[7] The Hebrew verb denotes physical desire (*e.g.* for food or drink) and thus here presumably refers to sexual attraction.
[8] Literally 'daughter of', which often means 'city of' or 'inhabitants of'. Possibly 'Tyre is mentioned as the last word in wealth (*cf.* Ezk. 27)' (Kidner).
[9] The reference here, as in the previous line, may be to the homage of other nations (*cf.* JB).
[1] With RSV I take this final phrase with verse 12 rather than with 13 (as in MT) (*cf.* the comments on 13, above).
[2] From Kidner's comments on the passage, p. 173.
[3] *Cf.* Dahood's translation.
[4] *I.e.* the arrows, presumably; but MT is jerky and the connection of thought unclear. Perhaps lines have changed places (*cf.* RSV, TEV). NEB, JB emend.
[5] *Awesome deeds* are always acts of God; *cf.* Ex. 34:10; Ps. 66:3, 5; Is. 64:3.

the more honour to the king; they prove that he is indeed God's vicegerent.

To this promise of glorious success are added further promises regarding the extent of his rule. First, as regards his own occupying of the throne of Israel:

The throne that God has given you[6] *will always be yours* (6).

Then, his rule will be extended through those sons whom he is invited to rejoice in as he becomes a father: *You will make them rulers throughout the world*[7] (16). The Davidic king was due to rule the world on Yahweh's behalf (*cf.* Ps. 2), and these sons will be the means of his exercise of this rule. And even beyond that, his name will be celebrated world wide beyond his own lifetime:

I will cause your name to be remembered to all generations:
Thus peoples will acknowledge you for all time (17).

KINGSHIP HUMAN AND DIVINE

Psalm 47 rejoices in the exaltation of Israel's divine King, Psalm 45 in the marriage of her human king, and they exemplify the many psalms concerned with the divine King or the human one. How are these two kingships related?

We have noted that the divine King came first; indeed, if you have God as King, do you have need (or room) for an earthly monarch? Certainly, when Israel asked for a human king, God read this as a rejection of his rule over them (1 Sa. 8:7). Nevertheless he let them have their wish. Indeed, he went the second and the third mile over the matter. The second mile was to involve himself in the election: if they were to have a king at all, he would see that they had the right one. The third mile was then to pledge himself in covenant with the kings, and to commit himself to working through them. He turns the expression of rebellion into the agency of obedience and the means of blessing.

Here is a paradigm example of God's condescending grace at work. He did not ask for a temple to be built; but if people felt

[6] TEV; the translation is discussed further, below.
[7] Or 'the land' (*cf.*, for instance, Rehoboam's action, 2 Ch. 11:22–23); but this is more prosaic.

there needed to be one, he would come and live there. He did not suggest a monarchy; but if they felt there needed to be one, he would work through it. He did not tell Adam to wear a loincloth; but if Adam felt he now needed to hide, God would provide him with a decent mohair suit (Gn. 3:21). God meets us where we are and adapts himself to our limitations. It is said that the craftsman who weaves a Persian carpet pushes his spindle across to an apprentice, who may not himself succeed in pushing it through in the right place; but if he goes wrong, the craftsman's genius is to be able to cope with his mistake and incorporate it into his pattern. So it is with God and his purpose in the world and the church.

Thus the human king comes to be blessed by God, anointed by God, commissioned by God to be the executive of his will in the world. The Old Testament does not think in terms of two kingdoms, of church and state supporting each other, but independent in their own spheres. There is only one kingdom; David's son sits on the throne of Yahweh's kingdom over Israel (1 Ch. 28:5).

Nevertheless, there are likely to arise tensions between God's will and harsh political, economic and social realities; and the latter generally win, as they are almost bound to do. Faith and righteousness yield to expediency and self-interest (or what seems to be expediency and self-interest). The kings generally fail to implement the justice of God and to inculcate trust in God in the threatening situations which occur; and running through the prophets is a twin note of condemnation for this failure. The kings were called to lead, but to lead under God.[8] Now when things go well, a body's leadership receives much of the credit; but if things go badly, the converse applies. The club manager's reputation is only as high as the most recent cup-replay entitles it to be. Normally, quality of leadership will be reflected in quality of performance. Thus the books of Kings explain Israel's failure and downfall, which came with the northern kingdom's defeat at

[8] Though without the legal authority of the monarchy, the leadership of the Christian church may find the correlation of these two psalms suggestive for an understanding of its ministry. Righteousness and trust remain among God's priorities, and those who exercise leadership among God's people are still responsible for them. They are called to leadership, but leadership under God, and they have authority only so long as they are following his lead.

the hand of the Assyrians and the southern kingdom's humiliation by the Babylonians, as the failure of the kings themselves. The human kingdom has cut loose from the divine kingdom. Anointing with oil, festivity and music and the splendour of ivory-panelling, which Psalm 45 rejoices in, become disassociated from a concern with the will of God, are condemned by the prophets (cf. Am. 6:4–6) and become the causes of defeat and exile.

Outwardly, however, the divine kingdom and the human kingdom still seem connected. The downfall of the human kingdom seems to imply the downfall of the divine kingdom. Thus in the exile Israel feels as though both her human king and her divine King have been deposed. The good news for the exiles, then, is the message of the one 'who says to Zion, "Your God is become King"' (Is. 52:7). His kingship has not been terminated. He has not been dethroned. 'Yahweh has reasserted his kingly rule, which might, even to his own people, have seemed in abeyance during the Babylonian domination.'[9]

The phrase from Isaiah is identical with that in Psalm 47:8, and the message of Isaiah 40–55 takes up many of the themes of the psalms and asserts that they are now to be made living realities again.[1] Earlier in Israel's history, we have assumed, the declaration that Yahweh was King stated the people's faith about present reality. But even then the assertion (and others about Israel's dominion over the nations) was presumably recognized as larger than life. Yahweh was not obviously exercising an effective rule over the whole world. Like the Christian who asserts that 'Jesus is Lord' even though the powers of evil do not in fact seem to acknowledge him, and even though much that happens to the believer and in the world generally seems unlikely to be part of his will, the Israelite declares 'Yahweh is King' and believes him to be Lord even when his lordship seems not to be realized. He makes this confession by faith; but he no doubt notices that it does not correspond to what his eyes see in the world.

The declaration that 'Yahweh reigns' is thus implicitly

[9] C. R. North, *The Second Isaiah* (The Clarendon Press, 1967), p. 222.

[1] Gunkel (p. 202) notes the connections between the motifs of 47:3–4 and those of Is. 14:2; 26:15; 27:6; 49:23; 54:3; 60:14; though he is inclined to date the psalms later.

forward-looking.[2] It is a statement of hope as well as one of faith. It is based on the lordship that Yahweh evidently has exercised in Israel's experience (as the confession of Jesus is based on the resurrection), but it is not satisfied with that; and with the exile, even this lordship seems to be suspended.

But Psalm 47 may be taken to refer to the future: *He shall subdue the people under us, and the nations under our feet. He shall choose our inheritance for us, the excellency of Jacob whom he loved* (3–4, AV). The statement of faith about the present becomes the statement of hope about the future.

In parallel with this, it was perhaps always widely realized that the grand descriptions of the *human* kings made them, too, larger than life. Certainly they do not fulfil the kingly ideal, and even in the lifetime of the monarchy prophets begin to look beyond the kings whom they can see to a future fuller realization of what God expects of kings (*e.g.* Is. 9:6–7; 11:1–5). The exile forces this forward orientation on the people as a whole. The word 'Messiah' will come to have its most familiar use not as a description of the king who is, but of the king who will be.

Thus the psalms which refer to Israel's king came to be understood in a Messianic sense: they expressed the Jews' hope of a future king, not their understanding of the position of a present king. This interpretation of Psalm 45 can be documented from the Targum, an interpretative paraphrase in Aramaic.[3] But it probably goes back into the Old Testament period and represents what such psalms would have meant to the Jews at the time when the Psalter was being compiled in the post-exilic period, when there were still no kings on the throne of Jerusalem. The king in Psalm 45 is the Messiah, and his bride is the people of God; Israel is often described as Yahweh's bride in the Old Testament (*e.g.* Is. 54:5–6; Je. 2–3; Ho. 1–3). Psalm 45 becomes a parable of

---

[2] Perhaps the word 'implicitly' is unnecessary, since the imperfect form of the Hebrew verb draws attention precisely to the unfinished nature of what is being spoken of. Certainly the ambiguity (from an English perspective) of the imperfect tense facilitates the psalm's being understood in a future-orientated way; see further, below.

[3] A targum, like *The Living Bible* today, not only translates but brings up-to-date, explains (*e.g.* obscure expressions) and re-interprets the text in the light of the beliefs of the translator and the way he understands the Bible as a whole. The written targums belong, as far as we know, to the Christian era, but they are assumed to embody oral paraphrase going back centuries.

this relationship, as too does the Song of Songs.[4] Both express the people's longing for the Messiah's marriage to his bride.

PSALM 45 AND PSALM 47 IN THE NEW TESTAMENT

It is not surprising that the New Testament regards the hope of a coming reign of the divine King and of a coming reign of a human king as fulfilled in Jesus. This is particularly clear in Hebrews 1. 'When he brings the firstborn into the world, God says, "Let all Gods angels worship him"' (Heb. 1:6) makes its point with an allusion to one of the psalms about God as King (97:7). Jesus brings the kingly presence of God himself, and he ought to be acknowledged as such. Two verses later, however, the writer to the Hebrews applies Psalm 45 to Christ. With regard to the Son, God says,

'Your throne, O God, is for ever and ever,
The righteous sceptre is the sceptre of your kingdom.
You have loved righteousness and hated lawlessness;
Therefore God, your God, has anointed you
With the oil of gladness beyond your comrades' (1:8-9, cf. RSV).

The first line of this quotation from the psalm is of uncertain translation, both in the psalmist's original and in the quotation in Hebrews. But if the RSV is right (the other translations are similar), then the verse from the psalm becomes Hebrews' most explicit testimony to the deity of Christ; and even if not, it expresses the writer's conviction that Jesus fulfilled the hopes both of the reign of God and of the reign of the Messiah.[5]

---

[4] As with the psalm, the Song of Songs was probably included in the canon as a parable of this relationship, even though it was first written as a love-poem.

[5] It is at least arguable, however, that RSV is wrong and that RSV mg. is the more natural understanding of the Greek: 'God is your throne for ever' (cf. NEB mg.), i.e., God is the support of your throne. The question of the correct translation of the Hebrew of Ps. 45:6a is even more difficult. 'Your throne, O God, is for ever and ever' is undoubtedly the natural translation. But who, if this is right, is being addressed? Hardly, in the context, God himself. But if the king is here addressed as God (as he is among other ancient Near

It may be that the rationale of applying these psalms to Jesus is not immediately obvious to us; or, alternatively, it may be that the necessity of concerning ourselves with the pre-exilic monarchy if the psalms were fulfilled in Jesus is the assumption that needs looking at. On the one hand, as far as we can tell, Psalm 45, for instance, was produced in response to one particular (though recurrent) historical situation, the wedding of Israel's king. But it was an inspired response. As we have noted, the psalmist does refer to his feeling of inspiration in the opening verse of his psalm. He cannot help but sing; he is almost like Jeremiah, when he cannot but speak his words of prophecy (Je. 20:9). And he seeks to bring to the situation to which he addresses himself not merely human good wishes and advice, but the divine perspective on this important moment for the king and his bride, and for the whole people. In so far as he succeeds in this aim, it is likely that his inspired words have more significance in them than merely what applies to an Israelite wedding. There will be more light to break forth from them than that. And the area upon which the psalm will throw its light is suggested by the later parts of the Old Testament and by the New, as we have seen: the king and his bride will have significance for the Messiah and his people, for Jesus and the church.

So, since God's word came in a particular human situation, we look at that situation seriously, for we have the privilege here of overhearing his word as it is addressed to particular men, and it is as we hear God speaking to the particular concerns of one situation that we may be able to understand what he says to others (such as our own). But we do not stop short at understanding the message in its origin in the past; we go on to try to grasp its significance in the light of what God has said since, and in particular in the light of Christ. To adapt an image which

---

Eastern peoples), then this is the only place in the OT where this happens. Perhaps it is an example of how what is said about the king is larger than life: he brings the presence and the rule of God (*cf.* Is. 7:14; 9:6; though these are both statements of hope about a future king). Kidner suggests that it should be translated in the straightforward way (*cf.* JB) and taken as 'an example of Old Testament language bursting its banks, to demand a more than human fulfilment'; and, while we may have to accept uncertainty as to the original (pre-exilic) meaning of the passage, this inference may be appropriate for the way the verse was read in the post-exilic period. It then deserves comparison with the directly Messianic passages from Is. 7 and 9 referred to above.

Spurgeon uses, it would be short-sighted to see only the king of Israel and his bride in Psalm 45; many biblical commentaries have stopped short at that, and consequently they seem to offer little help in achieving what they did ultimately aim at, namely the appropriation of the Bible's truth by the modern reader. On the other hand, it would be long-sighted to recognize here only Christ and the church; to be long-sighted is likely to result in falling over one's feet.[6] One needs, in fact, to be bifocal in one's approach, to see both Solomon and Jesus.[7]

Jesus is the one who resolves the tension between the two kingdoms. The origin of the monarchy lay in men's desire for a king they could see; it was not far from the plea, 'Give us a sign.' The plea is met in the incarnation, and we call the incarnate one Jesus *Christ*, Jesus the Messiah. The central affirmation we make about him, the category we use most often to describe him, is one that has its background in an act of rebellion against God as King. Here is that paradigm of God's mercy again: the act of rebellion is made the channel for the fulfilment of God's positive purpose of redemption in Jesus.

But there is more than that. The problem of the monarchy was the tension between the divine King and the human king. That tension is now resolved, however: the two kingships are combined in one person, who is the king of Israel but is also the one committed to his Father's will.

He is, of course, a new kind of king of Israel. '"The royal psalms show the rule and office of the anointed one in its—at present hidden—divine *doxa* [glory], which it has for itself already now, and which can become manifest any moment". . . .

---

[6] Spurgeon himself, for instance, takes the phrase *the king's daughter is all glorious within* (13) to refer to the beauty of the Christian's inward desires and character—as, indeed, did most commentators up to his time; *cf.* C. H. Spurgeon, *The Treasury of David* II (Passmore and Alabaster, 1883). pp. 357 f.; similarly, *e.g.*, D. Dickson, *The Psalms* (Banner of Truth, 1959; first published in 1653–55), p. 262. This seems forced.

[7] It is only fair to Spurgeon to acknowledge that I have re-worked his metaphor; what he actually says (p. 351) is, 'Some here see Solomon and Pharaoh's daughter only—they are short-sighted; others see both Solomon and Christ—they are cross-eyed; well-focused spiritual eyes see here Jesus only'; though he does grant the possibility of Solomon's shadow flitting across the screen (but without its having any significance for what God has to say through the psalm).

In the Old Testament this *doxa* has hidden itself more and more—until in Christ it has appeared *sub contrario crucis* [in the contradictory form of a cross], with the deepest veiling of all. The New Testament witnesses have believed it, however, and have recognized that beyond the hiddenness of the messiah, Jesus of Nazareth, the message of the Old Testament lights up aright for the first time, when the crucified one is raised up.'[8] Thus the majesty of Jesus in his lifetime is not triumphalist but meek:

> 'Ride on! ride on in majesty!
> In lowly pomp ride on to die;
> Bow Thy meek head to mortal pain,
> Then take, O God, Thy power, and reign.'

And if the psalm has implications for Christian leadership, then this aspect must be stressed, too. Leadership must be strong, but its strength is most clearly manifested when it suffers as it must.

Human kingship and divine kingship are thus manifested, with extraordinary diversity, in Christ's incarnation and ministry, in his death and resurrection, in his ascension and sitting at God's right hand. Now he is the church's Lord—her husband and master; she is his bride. Think of the commitment that a husband and wife make to each other: there you will see the commitment Christ makes to the church, and the responsive commitment he looks for from his bride.[9]

It is an odd kind of marriage, however, for bride and groom seem to be partly separated. Christ is King, but not all things are yet put into subjection to him. As the things that were said about the human kings in the Old Testament were larger than life, so, apparently, are the things that were said about Jesus in the New. We still live with the tension between the theological statement and the actuality, between the promise and its fulfilment. Like the men of the Old Testament, we live in hope of when God's kingdom *will* be realized, of when the bridegroom *will* come.

---

[8] Kraus, p. 21; the internal quotation is from von Rad, 'Erwägungen zu den Königspsalmen', *Zeitschrift für die alttestamentliche Wissenschaft* 58 (1940–41), pp. 219 f.

[9] See also Eph. 5:21–33, where Paul applies the analogy in the converse way: Christ's commitment to his people, and the one with which they respond, provides a model for the relationship of husband and wife.

The Spirit and the bride say 'Come'.
With your door open wide,
Won't you listen in the dark for the midnight cry,
And see that your light is on,
When the bridegroom comes?[1]

[1] From the song 'When the Bridegroom Comes' by David Omer Bearden, recorded by Judee Sill on the LP 'Heartfood' (E.M.I., 1973). The words allude to Mt. 25 and Rev. 22:17.

If God is with us
(Psalms 46, 48 and 50)

46   *The choirmaster's.   The Korahites'.   To Alamoth.   A song.*

¹ *We have God as a shelter and stronghold:*
  He always offers himself as a help in times of trouble.
² *Therefore we are not afraid of when the earth gives way,*
  Of when the mountains collapse into the depths of the sea:
³ *Let its waters rage and roar,*
  Let the mountains shake as it heaves!   Pause

⁴ *A river with its streams gladdens God's city,*
  The sacred dwelling of the Most High.
⁵ *God is in her midst; she will not collapse.*
  God will help her as morning dawns.
⁶ *Nations roar, kingdoms collapse;*
  He gives voice, the world melts.
⁷ *Yahweh Sabaoth is with us;*
  The God of Jacob is our high tower.   Pause

⁸ *Come and see what Yahweh has done.*
  He has brought total desolation on earth.
⁹ *He is putting an end to war through all the world.*
  He breaks the bow and snaps the spear,
  He burns the shields in the fire.
¹⁰ *Stop fighting, and acknowledge that I am God,*
  I will be supreme over the nations, supreme over the world

11 *Yahweh Sabaoth is with us;*
The God of Jacob is our high tower.   *Pause*

48 *A song.   A psalm.   The Korahites'.*

1 *Yahweh is great, and worthy of all praise*
In the city of our God.
2 *His sacred mountain is the beautiful height,*
The joy of the whole world.
Mount Zion is furthest Zaphon,
The Great King's city.
3 *In her fortresses God has proved himself as a high tower.*

4 *For the kings gathered together and advanced.*
5 *They looked, and then they were dumbfounded.*
They took fright and ran.
6 *They were seized by panic,*
They tossed like a woman in childbirth,
7 *As when the east wind wrecks Tarshish ships.*

8   *As we have heard, so have we seen,*
     In the city of Yahweh Sabaoth,
     In the city of our God.
     God establishes her for ever.   *Pause*

9 *We have re-presented how you kept your commitment, O God, within*
     your temple.
10 *As your name is known, O God, so your praise is sounded,*
To the ends of the earth.
You are armed with justice: Mount Zion rejoices;
11 *The cities of Judah are glad, because of your judgments.*

12 *Go about Zion, walk around her,*
Count her towers, note her rampart,
13 *Go through her strongholds,*
So that you can recount to the generation to come
14 *That this is God, our God for all time.*
He will guide us for ever.

50 *A psalm.   Asaph's.*

1 *The Mighty Lord, Yahweh, has spoken.*
He has summoned the world, from east to west.

² *From Zion, the city of perfect beauty,*
  God's light has shone forth.
³ *Our God is coming, he is not keeping silence.*
  Fire consumes before him, a storm rages around him.
⁴ *He summons heaven above, and the earth,*
  To the judgment of my people.
⁵ *Gather here those who committed themselves to me,*
  Those who made a covenant with me by sacrifice.
⁶ *Let the heavens declare his justice,*
  For God himself is giving judgment.   *Pause*

⁷ *Listen, my people, and I will speak.*
  Listen, Israel, and I will bear witness against you:
  I am God, your God.
⁸ *For your offerings I do not rebuke you,*
  Nor for your whole offerings, always before me.
⁹ *I would not take a bull from your home*
  Or a goat from your folds,
¹⁰ *For to me belongs every creature of the forest,*
  The cattle on the hills by the thousand.
¹¹ *I know every bird on the hills,*
  Everything that moves in the countryside is in my care.
¹² *If I get hungry, I would not tell you—*
  The world and all it contains are mine.
¹³ *Do I eat beef*
  And drink goats' blood?
¹⁴ *Make a thank-offering to God,*
  Fulfil your vows to the Most High.
¹⁵ *Call on me in time of trouble;*
  I will rescue you, and you will give me glory.

¹⁶ *But to the wicked man, God says:*
  What are you doing reciting my laws
  And speaking of my covenant?
¹⁷ *You are people who refuse my instruction*
  And throw off my words.
¹⁸ *Whenever you see a thief, you connive with him;*
  You associate with adulterers.
¹⁹ *You dedicate your mouth to evil,*
  You harness your tongue to deceit.

20 *You sit speaking against your brother,*
You slander your own mother's son.
21 *These are the things you have done: could I remain silent?*
You have planned people's ruin: could I be like you?
I will charge you, I will set out my case before you.
22 *Won't you see this, you who leave God out of account?*
Otherwise I will tear you to pieces, and there will be no-one to rescue
you.

23 *The man who brings a thank-offering honours me.*
To the man who orders his way, I will show the salvation of God.

We have noted, in discussing Psalms 45 and 47, that the problems of politics and religion and morality, described in the book of Judges, led to Israel having the human monarchy that God had not planned. The demands of this new form of government in turn led to her having a capital city and a fixed central shrine which do not seem to have been part of God's ideal either. Jerusalem was a Jebusite fortress, a city of dubious parentage; but God adopted it (Ezk. 16), he chose it (Ps. 132:13). The building of a temple in this city was originally David's idea, not God's; but God accepted the idea and made the temple his dwelling (see 2 Sa. 7; 1 Ki. 8). Henceforth 'the city of God' and 'the house of God' become central ideas in Old Testament thinking.

Through David's achievement as general and as king, Israel came to be a force to be reckoned with in the ancient Near East, and a capital city was a natural acquisition for his state and empire. Yet the antecedents for this city are worrying. 'The first builder of a city was Cain. . . . For God's Eden he substitutes his own . . . The next builder we hear of is Nimrod . . . The city is now a center from which war is raged. . . . A city marks man's every success. And a city must also mark the advance against God.'[1] And Jerusalem is by nature as much a city under the curse as any other city is. And yet 'it is in Jerusalem that we may find the foundation of the new Jerusalem'.[2]

The men who began to build the city of Babel included in their plans a tower, which is at least reminiscent of the ziggurats of

[1] J. Ellul, *The Meaning of the City* (ET, Eerdmans, 1970), pp. 1, 5, 10, 13, 16; cf. Gn. 4:17; 10:8–12; 11:4.
[2] Ellul, p. 110.

Sumeria. The object of building a ziggurat was to provide an artificial elevation which could be regarded as the dwelling-place of God; for gods were assumed to live on an elevated place, elsewhere an actual mountain or hill, which symbolized the cosmos itself ruled by God from its highest point—an elevated place which was 'the holy mountain of God' (Ezk. 28:14). There a temple would be built, there the god would be worshipped.[3]

Yahweh's holy mountain is first of all Mount Sinai; but, having appeared to Israel there, Yahweh accompanies her to Canaan and involves himself in her history, as he had done in rescuing her from Egypt. There is then a tension between the idea of a God who appears to his people at points in time, speaking to her and acting with her, and the idea of a God who is localized in some object,[4] or even at some particular place. As Yahweh accepted the city and made something of it, if only as a symbol for the future, so he accepts the temple and makes something of it. He does set up his abode there. But too often, like an image, the temple beguiles people into deluding themselves that they have God in their pocket: 'This is the temple of Yahweh, the temple of Yahweh, the temple of Yahweh' (Je. 7:4). In the end, the temple can be only a symbol, both negatively in its destruction, and positively in that it speaks of a purpose of God to dwell with his people. It is a purpose realized in Christ and in the Spirit, but the fate of the material temple reminds those who believe in Christ and are indwelt by the Spirit that God remains the God of history who casts things off and destroys them rather than be in anyone's pocket.

WE ARE NOT AFRAID? (Psalm 46)

We are not afraid of when the earth gives way,[5]
Of when the mountains collapse into the depths of the sea:
Let its waters rage and roar,
Let the mountains shake as it heaves! (2–3).

It may be that the Arctic ice-cap is melting, or could be made to

[3] On the content of this and the next paragraph, see, *e.g.*, R. E. Clements, *God and Temple* (Blackwell, 1964), especially chapters 1–4.

[4] *Cf.* the argument against images in Dt. 4:1–40.

[5] The verb *mûr* means 'to change'; the idea of losing stability could be an extension of this.

melt. The result of this eventuality would be the permanent flooding of London and other major cities. It may be that the sun is cooling down, or that less of its heat can penetrate our atmosphere. If this is so, it will lead eventually to crop-failure on a world scale and deaths from hypothermia. Anyone who lives in certain areas on the edge of the Indian Ocean lives in continual danger of the inundation of the ocean. Anyone who lives in San Francisco risks the destruction and death of earthquake.

We are not afraid? Of science fiction becoming fact? Of the realization that the stability of the world cannot be taken for granted?

Ancient peoples did not take the world's stability for granted. Perhaps the experience of earthquake and flood, of storm and whirlwind, against which they had less protection than we have, suggested that the cosmos embodied vast forces of energy barely restrained. Creation they in fact understood as the harnessing and controlling of these forces, to which quasi-personal existence was widely attributed. The creation of the world was the occasion of God's victory over chaos.

The Bible, too, utilizes this way of thinking, though its overall theology is different from that of the Babylonians or the Canaanites; it, too, speaks of the sea as the very embodiment of the forces of chaos.[6] But it regards the world as securely founded:

'He has founded it upon the seas, and established it upon the rivers' (Ps. 24:2).
'The world is established; it shall never be moved' (Pss. 93:1; 96:10).

The Genesis creation story contains few references to this way of understanding creation; it appears more in the poetry of the Bible. For the Bible, too, does accept that the seething dynamic of the forces put under restraint by God may seem to threaten to break out again. Nevertheless they remain under his control:

'The floods have lifted up, Yahweh,
The floods have lifted up their voice,
The floods lift up their roar.
Mightier than the noise of many waters,
Mightier than the sea's breakers,
Mighty on high is Yahweh!' (Ps. 93:3–4).

[6] Cf. the comments on 42:6–7, above, pp. 30 f.

These powers are under his control and available for his use. They were on one occasion unleashed, and 'all the springs of the great deep broke through' (Gn. 7:11); but God then promised 'never again' (Gn. 9:11, 15), and that promise remains the guarantee of the stability of the cosmos.

The floods apparently threaten to break through again, however. They assert themselves against God.[7] They strive to turn cosmos back into chaos. But *we are not afraid*. How in such a situation can we be free from fear? Because *we have God as a shelter*[8] *and stronghold* (1).

The image of a shelter, or stronghold or citadel (1, 7, 11), is an important one in Israelite thinking. To be more accurate, several pictures are here interwoven. We have already noted the idea of God as a rock (42:9), the one to whom we cling when the floods threaten to sweep us to destruction. The notion of shelter from rain or storm is familiar enough in most climates, and this is part of the background of the word *shelter* here (*cf.* Jb. 24:8; Is. 4:6; 25:4). In Palestine, however, men find themselves at least as often seeking shelter from the sun with its dangerous heat (*cf.* Jdg. 9:15; Is. 30:2).

Citadels and strongholds and towers speak most loudly, however, of refuge from military pressures. Palestine was in Old Testament times, as it is now, a cockpit of world history. Darius and Alexander, Saladin and Napoleon, Allenby and Kissinger are beyond our period; the Philistines and the Syrians, the Egyptians and the Moabites, the Assyrians and the Babylonians are not. Palestine's political history was a tale of invasion, war and destruction, as the archaeological remains of Palestinian cities reveal. These cities, Hazor and Megiddo, Gezer and Shechem, Mizpah and Lachish, are notable indeed not for their beauty or for their treasures but for their fortifications: double walls, concealed water-systems, sometimes (as at Shechem) with a citadel

[7] Note especially the expression *as it heaves* in Ps. 46:3b; more literally *with its tumult* (RSV). The noun can suggest both excellence or majesty, and the confidence and assertiveness which are appropriate to majesty—though they may become sinful pride and self-assertiveness (*cf.* Pss. 31:18, 23; 36:11). The noun here, then, suggests the sea's physical rising which is taken as expressive of a personal assertiveness, and which threatens to overwhelm the inhabited land (*cf.* Ps. 89:9; Jb. 38:11). These parallels suggest that the sea's mightiness, not God's (NEB), is referred to here; the latter comes later (6–11).

[8] More literally, 'God is for us a shelter . . . .'.

within the citadel. Here the peoples of the countryside around sought refuge when news came of the approach of Sennacherib or Nebuchadnezzar, as earlier of Joshua or David. Here men sought safety and protection, hoping that the enemy would not bother to sit out a siege.

With a glance at these physical protections, the psalmists sing of God as their shelter and their refuge and their citadel:

'I love you, Yahweh, my strength.
Yahweh is my rock, my fortress, and my rescuer.
My God is my rock in whom I find refuge,
My shield, the hill where I find safety,[9] my high tower.
I call on Yahweh as the one to whom praise is due,
And I am saved from my enemies' (Ps. 18:1–3).

God does not guarantee that trouble will not come to those who trust in him. But he does guarantee that, when trouble comes, he will be the rock that saves us, the citadel that protects us, the tower that frustrates our enemies.

Israel was in fact always tempted to look elsewhere for protection, to trust in human strength. In the time of Isaiah she sought shelter in alliances with the Egyptians, whom she trusted to protect her against the Assyrians. This, however, was to take refuge, to seek shelter, in what was false. Yahweh's call was for Israel to trust in him (Is. 28:15–16), to say, in fact, *We have God as a shelter and stronghold*. Israel was inclined to 'go down to Egypt for help' and to rely on horses and chariots, forgetting that 'the Egyptians are men, and not God, and their horses flesh, and not spirit' (Is. 31:1–3). Yahweh's call to Israel is that she should testify that God *always offers himself*[1] *as a help in times of trouble* (Ps. 46:1).

The pressures of history

The psalm's opening verses speak explicitly of the disasters of nature, but its imagery suggests also the pressures of history. This

[9] *Cf.* NEB; other EVV have 'the horn of my salvation' or the like. But 'horn' is a way of speaking of a hill in Is. 5:1 (so also in Arabic, according to BDB), and this meaning fits well here.

[1] Literally 'lets himself be found'. *Cf.* Is. 55:6, 'seek Yahweh while he is letting himself be found'; 2 Ch. 15:4, 'in trouble . . . they sought him, and he let himself be found by them'.

reference becomes explicit in verses 4–6: many of the expressions of the psalm's opening verses recur, with this different idea in mind. The roar of the sea becomes the roar of the nations, the collapse of the mountains becomes the collapse of the kingdoms (6): though there will be no collapse of God's city, for he is its help (5). The world does not merely give way as the chaos powers assert themselves; it falls apart in fear when God acts.

If the instability of nature is (or ought to be) a reality to the mind of the twentieth-century man, then he may need even less reminder of the pressures of history. The crises that threaten us change—from Vietnam and Nigeria to Angola and the Lebanon to whatever further volcanoes are brewing. But the change is only outward, only in the location of the trouble. The reality of wars and rumours of wars is a consistent one. *Nations roar, kingdoms collapse* (6).

The psalmist knew this experience, too. Zion did not escape these pressures. But *she will not collapse* (5). The psalmist utilizes two images in declaring that she is safe. First,

> *A river with its streams gladdens God's city,*
> *The sacred dwelling of the Most High* (4).

There is in fact a stream that provided water for Jerusalem: indeed the Arabs of Silwan still do their washing in it and irrigate their gardens from it. The gentle Siloam ran from the Gihon spring and, at least from the time of Hezekiah's tunnelling work (2 Ki. 20:20; 2 Ch. 32:30), filled a pool inside the city walls, referred to in the New Testament as 'the pool of Siloam' (Jn. 9:7). In Isaiah's day, Israel despised these waters in her fear of the Syrians, and for this sin Yahweh determined to send against her the floods of a much greater river, the Euphrates—which represents the power of the Assyrians, much more threatening than the mere Syrians (Is. 8:5–8). It seems that the waters of Siloam symbolized Yahweh's unspectacular provision and protection of his people, as the mighty Euphrates symbolized the might of the Assyrians as the historical embodiment of the chaos powers.

In Psalm 46, too, there is a contrast between the destructive, roaring, seething waters of the sea, with its arrogant self-assertiveness, and the refreshment of *a river with its streams,* which remind us of the ones which watered the garden that God planted at the beginning of the human story (Gn. 2:10–13).[2] They point us on also to the water flowing from the temple mount in Ezekiel's vision (Ezk. 47) and the river of the water of life flowing from God's throne in the New Jerusalem (Rev. 22:1–2). The river suggests God's provision. It links his heavenly home with the earthly hill on which he deigns to dwell. Here is reason for confidence that the storms of nature and of history will not be overwhelming: the waters of a gentler river refresh this place, because it is the sacred dwelling of God. If only his people will trust him, they will find that 'there Yahweh in majesty will be for us a place of broad rivers and streams' (Is. 33:21).

The second image whereby the psalmist justifies his assurance that Zion is safe is very different: it is that of God the warrior.

> *God is in her midst; she will not collapse.*
> *God will help her as morning dawns* (5).

The phrase *as morning dawns* recalls the Israelites' victory at the Reed Sea, when the waters returned to engulf the Egyptians 'as morning dawned' (Ex. 14:27). It recalls the slaughter of the Assyrian army encamped before Jerusalem, discovered 'when men arose early in the morning' (2 Ki. 19:35). The break of dawn is the time of battle. Night-time is generally safe: it is a time for relaxing, a good time for a stratagem (Jdg. 7), but not the time for an orthodox attack. The coming of the morning is the time when the besieged city is likely to find itself under attack.

There may also be a contrary flavour to the expression. The coming of morning is usually welcome. Night may be safe, but men do not like darkness and normally prefer light. Darkness speaks of misery and disaster; morning and light suggest salvation. Sin means distress and darkness, gloom and thick darkness, without dawn; grace means that the people who walked in darkness see a great light (Is. 8:20–9:2). Yahweh's day is expected to be light, but because of sin it will be darkness (Am. 5:18–20). The watchman is anxiously asked, 'What is left of the night?' He answers, reassuringly but petulantly and sombrely, 'Morning is coming—though night will follow it again' (Is. 21:11–12). The

---

[2] Which included Euphrates and Gihon!

passage is not just an excerpt from everyday life, but a message to Israel in a dark night of distress.[3]

For God's city dawn is, in fact, the moment of decision. It is potentially the moment of salvation, but possibly the moment of disaster. At this crucial moment, and as the *nations roar* and *kingdoms collapse*, God *gives voice* and *the world melts* in fear before him (6): for

> Yahweh Sabaoth is with us;
> The God of Jacob is our high tower[4] (7).

It is precisely *Yahweh Sabaoth* who is the warrior God. He is 'Yahweh of armies' who leads the forces of heaven and earth, 'the Almighty Yahweh'.[5] Such a description might well alarm us; but the psalmist takes it as a comfort, because this mighty God is on our side. His presence means that, even when we are outwardly outnumbered, 'those who are with us are more than those who are with them': all we need is eyes to see the fact (2 Ki. 6:15–17). Or, as the psalmist himself puts it, *Yahweh Sabaoth* is also *the God of Jacob*, the one who has entered into a relationship with the family of Abraham.

'That our faith may rest truly and firmly in God, we must take into consideration at the same time these two parts of his character—his immeasurable power, by which he is able to subdue the whole world under him; and his fatherly love which he has manifested in his word. When these two things are joined together, there is nothing which can hinder our faith from defying all the enemies which may rise up against us.'[6]

Here is a profound faith, that 'a testimony is borne to God in the

[3] *Cf.* O. Kaiser's comments in *Isaiah* 13–39 (ET, Old Testament Library, SCM Press, 1974), p. 131.

[4] *miśgāḇ* comes from a verb which means 'to be inaccessibly high'. It is used of material citadels (Is. 25:12) as well as of spiritual defences (Ps. 48:3), which mean we will not be moved (Ps. 62:2, 6).

[5] The precise meaning of the title *Yahweh Sabaoth* is much discussed, but without certain conclusions (see Anderson, pp. 205 f.); the general implication of the name is clear, however. *ṣᵉḇā'ôṯ* is the ordinary Hebrew word for armies (see on 44:9, above, p. 60).

[6] From Calvin's comments on Ps. 46:7.

jubilant tones of a hymn, though it is related to an event of which man can think only with terror in his heart'.[7]

We shall have cause to note, in connection with Psalm 50, that the belief that 'God is with us' is a dangerous doctrine. Assurance easily becomes presumption. It is, nevertheless, a doctrine we could not live without: *Yahweh is with us.*

Come and see

Come and see what Yahweh has done . . . (8). Where is the psalmist inviting his people to look? Where do they behold the achievements of God?

The works of the Lord were visible in history. At the Reed Sea, Israel 'saw the great power with which Yahweh acted against the Egyptians' (Ex. 14:31); and recurrently come the reminders: 'You have seen all that Yahweh did before your eyes . . .' (Dt. 29:2); 'you have seen all that Yahweh your God has done . . .' (Jos. 23:3). Closer to the psalmist is what Israel saw at the time of Sennacherib's invasion of Judah in 701, and there are many parallels between the message of Isaiah in that situation and the language of this psalm.[8] At the very least, the psalmist and Isaiah belonged to circles that did their theology in similar terms; indeed, if any psalm can best be understood as a response to a particular historical situation, then this is one. It invites the people of the world to 'come and see' what Yahweh has now done for Israel.

But what would 'come and see' mean for subsequent generations, for later Israelites who sang this psalm without having experienced this particular deliverance? The invitation is, of course, one issued in worship (*cf.* those in Ps. 66:5, 16),[9] and it is parallel to the 'O come, all ye faithful . . . Come and behold Him' of our Christmas (and Easter) hymns. For the Israelite, or Christian, congregation, the great acts of God are not just something past. They are real now as we recall and relive them; they affect our lives now. Thus the life of worship feeds faith.

The vision of which the psalmist speaks looks beyond what can be literally seen, however.

[7] Weiser, p. 369.
[8] See especially Is. 33.
[9] See also the comments on 48:9, below, p. 117.

> Yahweh *has brought total desolation*[1] *on earth.*
> *He is putting an end to war through all the world.*
> *He breaks the bow and snaps the spear,*
> *He burns the shields*[2] *in the fire* (8–9).

The scene is one of the devastation of those seething nations, but 'the destruction serves a higher purpose. It is true that broken bows, shattered spears and burned shields lie about at the end of the road which man must walk if he relies on his own power, but at the same time they are also present at the beginning of the way which mankind is to enter upon according to God's purpose. They testify to God's will for peace, who wants to make all wars in the world to cease for ever'[3] (*cf.* Is. 2:4; 9:5; Ezk. 39:9–10).

But we know only too well that this is still a vision, not literal present reality. Within sight of the Jerusalem of Hezekiah and Isaiah's day is a 'peace-memorial', a sculpture embodying the turning of swords into ploughshares; but it overlooks a valley that Jordan and the Palestinians still regard as merely the cease-fire line between Arabs and Israelis, overrun by the Israelis in 1967. The State of Israel herself, while seeking peace, channels 40% of her gross national product into the manufacture of bow, spear and shield: fighter plane, atom bomb and radar screen. And the Middle East is only a paradigm of the nations' situation as a whole, far from the vision described by the psalmist.

It is in fact characteristic of Old Testament worship (and of ours) not only to look back, to the historic acts of God, but also to look beyond them to the complete consummation of what they point to, which is not yet an experienced reality, but which is presaged in what we do actually experience. 'Come and see' denotes the use not just of the physical eyes, but of spiritual vision.

What vision sees is that Yahweh is not only a means of escape from pressures and trials. He is also Lord over them. He is not an escape from history, but the one who is working out his purpose

---

[1] Like English words such as 'desolation' or 'shock', *šammah* can signify both material devastation and consequent personal appalled horror. The noun is plural (*cf.* RSV), and may thus suggest 'total desolation'.

[2] *caḡālôṭ* means 'carts', not 'chariots' (RSV), which are out of place in war and (being iron-made) difficult to burn. Hence the revocalization *caḡilôṭ*, 'shields' (a word otherwise known only from Aramaic).

[3] From Weiser's comments on 46:9.

in history. And he is therefore not just a Saviour to be trusted, but also a Lord to be acknowledged. Thus, the psalmist goes on: *Stop fighting, and acknowledge that I am God* (10; *cf.* TEV). 'Be still, and know that I am God' sounds a little too refined. It suggests an atmosphere of meditation and quiet. But this command is one uttered in history by the God of history, who, as he sees men presuming to work their own will out in history, says 'Stop!'. His firm command reminds one of his rebuke and scorn of the nations conspiring against Yahweh and his anointed (Ps. 2:1–4).

I will be supreme over the nations, supreme over the world (10). The presence and support of Yahweh Sabaoth has implications not just for now but for the final victory of God.

'A safe stronghold'

It would be difficult to leave Psalm 46 without a reference to Martin Luther's *Ein feste Burg*, his hymn based loosely on Psalm 46 but expressive of his own faith and experience—to which also he called the reforming church of the 1520s. It is said that John Wesley, too, used the words of this psalm's refrain as his comfort as he faced his death.[4] What the psalm meant to these individuals reminds us that its declarations of faith speak not only when creation or history seem to be in turmoil, but when our personal world seems to collapse. What shall I do if I am made redundant? What if my marriage breaks up? What shall I do when my mother dies? What if my husband has to give up work? I might fail my exams. How can I protect my daughter from the moral pressures of the age? What if my son gets in with a bad lot of friends? How, then, can we say *we are not afraid*? Because it is still true that

> *Yahweh Sabaoth is with us;*
> *The God of Jacob is our high tower.*

'God is with us.' The phrase is taken up by Isaiah (7:14; 8:8, 10). From him it is carried further and becomes a keynote especially in Matthew's Gospel. The first of Matthew's very many quotations from the Jewish Bible takes up one of these passages from Isaiah: the baby to be born of Mary is 'Emmanuel (which means, God with us)' (1:23). 'God with us' does not stop with the life of Jesus, however. He himself promises that 'where two

[4] *Cf.* Prothero, pp. 304 f.

or three are gathered together in my name, there am I in their midst' (18:20); and at the very end of the Gospel the risen Christ further declares, 'I am with you' to the end of time (28:20). The presence of Christ brings the presence of God. If Christ is with us, then God is with us. And he is with us in all the challenges and crises that will come to us as a result of our involvement in his work in the world.

GLORIOUS THINGS OF THEE ARE SPOKEN
(Psalm 48)

Like Psalm 46, Psalm 48 is a hymn of praise, and more specifically one of 'the songs of Zion' (*cf.* Ps. 137:3), which praise God for all that Jerusalem meant to Israel. Verses 1–7 concentrate on the objective side of the significance of Zion: it is the city which belongs to Yahweh (1–3), the city where he won the victory over the world powers (4–7). Here is its theological/historical meaning. The second half of the psalm takes up the subjective side of the significance of Zion: it is the city where we have seen God's love for ourselves (9–11) and which will speak of his protection for future generations also (12–14). Here is the meaning of Zion as it comes home to present and future generations.

Four four-line stanzas,[5] then, expound the importance of Zion. They are themselves summed up in the middle verse of the psalm (8), which we omitted from the analysis above. Here each line encapsulates the theme of a stanza:

> *As we have heard, so have we seen* (the theme of 9–11)
> *In the city of Yahweh Sabaoth*[6] (the theme of 4–7)
> *In the city of our God* (the theme of 1–3)
> *God establishes her for ever* (the theme of 12–14)

Thus verse 8, at the heart of the psalm, expresses its four stanzas in a nutshell.

The four stanzas are woven together by one further link: references to the four points of the compass. The first refers to the

---

[5] The balance of these four stanzas is reflected in the modern translations (see especially JB, TEV).

[6] In that this title of God describes him as the one who wins all the battles he enters; *cf.* the comments on 44:9; 46:7, above, p. 60, 106.

north (2), and the second to the *east* (7): these allusions come out clearly in most of the English translations.[7] The other allusions are easier to miss, since they derive from the way the Israelites thought of the points of the compass. The word for *east* (7) means literally 'in front': apparently, when the Israelite thought out the points of the compass, he did so facing east (presumably, that is, beginning where the sun rose). Thus he spoke of east and west, north and south, as 'in front of you', 'behind you', 'on your left hand' and 'on your right hand'. Now, in this psalm, the third stanza refers to God's *right hand* (10; *cf.* RSV), and the fourth to people 'behind' us[8] (13). It seems unlikely that this is a coincidence: these two phrases complete the four stanzas' references to the four points of the compass.[9] By this means the poet declares the total Lordship of the God of Israel. He is the God of the north (2), of Zaphon[1] where the Canaanites located God's dwelling-place; the God of the east, of the wind that comes from before you (7); the God whose right hand is working out his just purposes (10); and the God whom even the people behind us, whom we cannot yet see (13), will also be able to rely on and will be obliged to acknowledge.

Job, in his desperate search for God, declared:

'If I go eastward, he is not there;
If I go to the west, I cannot discern him;
When he acts in the north, I cannot see him;
He hides in the south and I cannot behold him' (Jb. 23:8–9).[2]

---

[7] Except the TEV and Gelineau versions of verse 2.

[8] The Israelites thought of the future as lying behind them (because it cannot yet be seen) and of the past as lying in front of them (because it can be seen and understood in a way that the future cannot): life involves being the oarsman, not the cox! (*Cf.* J. N. Schofield, *Introducing Old Testament Theology*, SCM Press, 1964, pp. 26 f.) Thus, here, generations still to come (RSV *the next generation*) are spoken of as 'behind' us.

[9] I owe this understanding of the structure of the psalm to M. Palmer, 'The Cardinal Points in Psalm 48', in *Biblica* 46:3 (1965), pp. 357 f.

[1] The word for 'north' in verse 2; it refers to a sacred mountain in Syria. Another way of referring to the points of the compass was to speak of places that lay in the four directions: Mount Zaphon, the desert, the Negeb, the (Mediterranean) Sea.

[2] *Cf.* JB for the recognition that the points of the compass are referred to here.

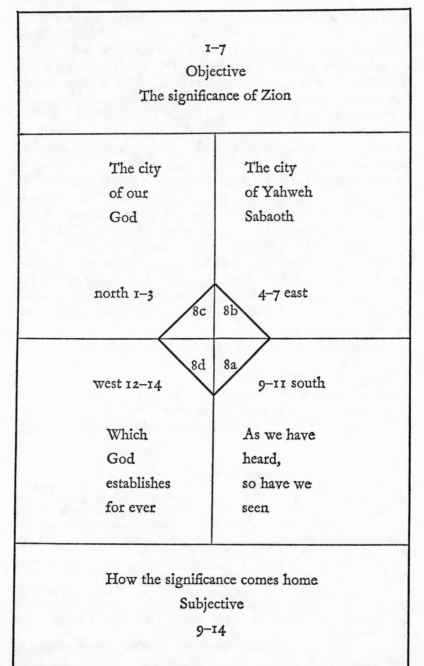

1–7
Objective
The significance of Zion

The city
of our
God

The city
of Yahweh
Sabaoth

north 1–3

8c | 8b

4–7 east

8d | 8a

west 12–14

9–11 south

Which
God
establishes
for ever

As we have
heard,
so have we
seen

How the significance comes home
Subjective
9–14

'In whatever direction I look, I cannot find him.' Sometimes that is how it feels. But the psalmist says, 'He is there, nevertheless; north and south, east and west, all belong to him.' Wherever I go, he is in fact there (*cf.* Ps. 139:7–12).

Zion, city of our God (verses 1–3)

Yahweh is great, and worthy of all praise. The title 'hymns of Zion' for psalms such as 46 and 48, which sing of the splendour of Jerusalem, is apposite, and yet it could be misleading. They are not quite the same as the moving Israeli song written after the 1967 war, 'Jerusalem the Golden'. They are not concerned to glory in a certain city, but to glory in a certain God. When the Old Testament does glory in Jerusalem, or in creation, or in the law, or in events of history, it does so as a way of praising the God who stands behind these realities. Psalm 48 makes this point clear in its opening testimony, that *Yahweh* is to be praised—*in the city of our God.*

Nevertheless, what is so special about this particular city? Six further phrases are used to describe it.[3]

> *His sacred mountain is the beautiful height,*
> *The joy of the whole world.*
> *Mount Zion is furthest*[4] *Zaphon,*
> *The Great King's city* (2).

Each of these triple descriptions of the city begins with an empirical fact on which there would be no disagreement: we are concerned with a city on a mountain sacred to Yahweh, and its name is the hill of Zion.[5] But the remaining descriptions of this

---

[3] The six noun-phrases in fact follow each other without verbs or prepositions (or punctuation, of course, originally) to indicate how they are to be linked together. I take them as two threes (as in fact do RSV and JB, though they punctuate the sentence differently; *cf.* also *BHS*).

[4] The word is actually a construct plural noun, which is usually translated 'furthest parts' or 'deepest parts'; *cf.* NEB, JB.

[5] Zion was the name of the Jebusite fortified city captured by David, which then became David's city; 'Jerusalem' covered a broader area around 'Zion'. The situation is in fact the same now, though the hill now called 'Mount Zion' is further west than the hill originally referred to by this name. But generally in the Old Testament Jerusalem and Zion are treated as equivalents (*e.g.* Is. 40:9).

city embody claims that every Canaanite would dispute: he would not accept that *Yahweh*'s city deserved these epithets, as the psalmist claims.

The beautiful height. At the northern end of Mount Carmel, on Israel's Mediterranean coast, a road runs along the edge of a ridge where the mountain falls headlong into Haifa town. There is a spectacular view of the city sprawled at your feet, of the traffic visible but not audible, of the bay and the harbour. The road is called 'Yaphe Nof', and it is the same expression which is used here: 'beautiful height'.

Jerusalem, however, is not really like that. The books say that no-one can fail to be moved by his first sight of Jerusalem. But most people nowadays get their first sight of the city as they drive up a dual carriageway, tankers rumbling up the inside lane, and Israeli buses thundering up the outside lane as if last week they were on exercises in Sinai (which they were). If you dare to take your eyes off the road, your first sight of Jerusalem is a housing estate, which, apart from the fact that it is on the top of a hill, might belong to any city.

Nor was the Jerusalem of Old Testament times very significant: not as high, for instance, as the Mount of Olives to the east. It was not geographically very significant, that is. If it was *the beautiful height, the joy of the whole world,* this was not so much an estimate of its physical characteristics as of its religious significance. For this is where heaven and earth meet, where God meets man, where the gulf between Creator and creature, and between holiness and the sinner, is bridged. This is a mountain whose top reaches heaven, one which means everything to the man who seeks God there. Physically impressive the hills of Bashan (the Golan Heights and Mount Hermon) may be, but they look with envy at the hill where the Lord delights to dwell (Ps. 68:15–16). Because Yahweh is there, it is *the beautiful height, the joy of the whole world.*[6]

Further, *Mount Zion is furthest Zaphon.* Again, this is not so, in the literal sense. But the Canaanites located the dwelling of God on the remote northern height of this mountain; and the psalmist declares that, on the contrary, the little hill of Zion is in reality the mountain of God. Perhaps there is, further, the implication that

[6] See, further, the introduction to this chapter, above, on the significance of Zion and of the temple there.

it is not far away and difficult of access. It is here. It fulfils the function which the Canaanites ascribe to Zaphon. And it is also *the Great King's city*. There seems to be another polemical point involved in this claim. The monarch of Assyria, Israel's overlord for much of the pre-exilic period, described himself as 'the great king'. On the contrary, says the psalmist, the great king is Yahweh. Indeed he has proved it to Israel: *in her fortresses God has proved himself as a high tower* (3). She has outwardly impressive buildings;[7] but her real strength lies in Yahweh.

Zion, the city of Yahweh Sabaoth (verses 4–7)

The second stanza develops the theme introduced by verse 3, the theme of Yahweh's victories won in this city. It recalls how

> *The kings gathered together and advanced.*
> *They looked, and then they were dumbfounded.*
> *They took fright and ran.*
> *They were seized by panic,*
> *They tossed like a woman in childbirth,*
> *As when the east wind wrecks Tarshish ships.*[8]

They came, they saw . . . But then suddenly there is the great reversal: not 'they conquered', but 'they fled'.[9]

What they saw that was so shattering, what caused the reversal, we do not now know. There is a mystery at the heart of the story. Somehow they found themselves face to face with the power of God, and somehow they found that they had turned tail and run for their lives. The passage is reminiscent of the story of how the people of Nazareth took Jesus to the top of another hill to throw him off to his death, but then watched him pass through the midst of them as they were somehow unable to bring their plan to fruition (Lk. 4:29–30). There is a similar mystery here: the power of evil finds itself unable to execute its will. 'A nod alone on the part of God is sufficient to deliver us.'[1]

[7] They could be palaces (NEB, JB) or citadels (RSV, TEV).

[8] Where Tarshish was is uncertain, but it was a long way, and thus the vessels capable of this voyage were notable for their size and strength (*cf.* Is. 2:16). But before a gale they may be destroyed like matchwood; and so it is with the proud strength of Israel's attackers when confronted by Yahweh.

[9] *Cf.* Calvin's comments on this passage.

[1] Again from Calvin's comments on 48:4–6.

But what is the incident to which the psalmist is referring? We have noted above in connection with Psalm 46 that, despite appropriate hesitation today over connecting psalms with specific historical events, that psalm seems to have inextricable links with the crisis that came to Judah in the time of Sennacherib, and the same is true with this very similar psalm. If it is more likely that the preacher quotes the hymn-book than the other way round, then perhaps we may picture Isaiah taking up the language and ideas of such psalms and promising the people that the declarations of faith which they made when they sang these psalms would indeed be vindicated.

And it was. There in the eighth century the forces that oppose God found their earthly representative in the Assyrians who attacked Jerusalem, and whose threat mysteriously dissolved into nothing (2 Ki. 19). That was a particular example of what the psalm describes. The people of God are ever under pressure from the world, but they do experience deliverance.

For us, it may not be military oppression. It may be the unseen pressure of suffering, or the forces of secularism. Behind it all are the forces of evil, and these may often seem to have stormed the very gates of Jerusalem. But God's people experience deliverance. They also look forward to a final deliverance and a final destruction of the powers of evil, a hope not without foundation but based on the fact that the final victory pushes its way into life now and makes its presence felt in the victories we already have. This was the experience of God's people in Hezekiah's day; it is ours, too, as God again in our lives adds to the catalogue of his mighty deeds.

As we have heard, so have we seen (verses 9-11)

The psalmist celebrates the glory of Zion (1-3), the place where victory has been won (4-7). But how is it that his picture of this victory is so vivid? On the view that the psalm was written to celebrate the victory over Sennacherib, that is easy to understand: this is the vividness of the herald fresh from the scene of battle. But even if the psalm was written on this occasion, we may ask how the words came to later singers. How do they see and hear of what the Lord has done (8)?

We have re-presented[2] how you kept your commitment,[3] O God,
  within your temple (9).

It seems that the Israelites not only read about the great acts of
God and talked about them in their families, though they did
both of these. They also, apparently, in some way dramatized
them and thus by another means brought them home to themselves. They have seen with their own eyes in the worship of the
temple, perhaps in a way analogous to the Christian's seeing with
his own eyes at the Lord's Supper, as he visually, physically and
dramatically recalls what God has done for him in Christ.

Often the human desire for the visual and dramatic has led the
church astray in worship. And yet, near the centre of our religious
life, is the symbolic drama in which we re-enact the story of
God's love, when we break bread together. The Lord's Supper is
more than an audio-visual aid, but it includes that function; and,
with psalms such as 46 and 48, provides every encouragement for
efforts to bring home in drama and dance the story of what God
has done for us.

The end of it all is that God himself is acknowledged, however.

As your name is known, O God, so your praise is sounded,
To the end of the earth (10).

One check on whether the drama is fulfilling its real purpose is
the question whether it is leading to a wider and deeper glorying
in God's name. There is a further check even on that worship, for
it is not to become pietistic. Lest it should be so, the psalmist goes
on to remind us of what it is about God that makes him deserve
worship:

You are armed[4] with justice:[5] Mount Zion rejoices;

  [2] *Cf.* NEB. The verb is generally taken to mean 'think about', 'meditate on',
but there is no clear parallel for this meaning, and 'produce an image or
resemblance', 're-enact', fits the verb's meaning elsewhere and fits the context
here well.

  [3] The clause translates the noun *ḥesed,* 'your covenant-loyalty' (see on 51:1,
below, pp. 159 ff.).

  [4] Literally 'your right hand is full': the expression can refer to being
equipped with something (*e.g.* 2 Sa. 23:7).

  [5] *ṣedeq,* one of the most interesting theological words in the Old Testament,
with a wide range of meanings in connection with what is 'right'. It can refer

The cities[6] of Judah are glad, because of your judgments[7] (11).

Joy and gladness stem from justice and judgment! The people of God rejoice in that righteousness of God which makes him act righteously and fulfil a righteous purpose in the world—a righteous purpose which will mean triumph for his people when their enemies wrongly oppress them or when they are themselves the means of his bringing judgment upon God's enemies, but which will also mean receiving judgment themselves when they go against him. And the people of God are glad about God's acts of judgment, those moments when he exercises his authority and makes his decisions and effects his will—decisions which will again mean triumph for his people when they are right with him, but may mean trouble when they themselves deserve judgment. But so long as Israel stays with God, then justice and judgment are the same thing as the keeping of God's commitment of which the psalmist spoke earlier (9). They mean that God is actively on their side as their defender and vindicator.

God establishes her for ever (verses 12–14)

The psalm's final stanza moves on from the praise the people offer now in the temple, to the building up of their faith so that they can pass it on to future generations. Developing one's faith can equip one to share it with others.

---

to the 'correct' way to do something (see Ps. 51:19), but more characteristically, of course, denotes what is morally correct or 'righteous' (see 45:7). This *ṣedeq*, however, is a matter not just of inner character, but of outward behaviour in the world which expresses itself in a concern that what is right shall be done. This concern will inevitably involve conflict, and thus *ṣedeq* refers to the kind of right action that triumphs over evil in the conflict for justice. EVV thus use the word 'victory' to translate *ṣedeq* (see Ps. 48:10, JB; also Is. 41:2, 10; *etc*.), though this is really too narrow a translation in that it does not bring out the idea of the triumph of right which belongs to the word *ṣedeq*.

6 More literally 'daughters'; cf. on 45:12, above, p. 86.

7 *mišpāṭ*, a word whose meaning overlaps with *ṣedeq* in so far as it is connected with justice, and with the triumphing of justice and of Yahweh's purpose in the world. This theme, like the parallel connotation of *ṣedeq*, comes to clearest expression in Isaiah 40–55 (*e.g.* 40:27; 42:1). But the underlying idea behind the root *š-p-ṭ* is probably that of the exercise of authority in decision-making, not that of judging: God's effecting of his *mišpāṭ* is his realizing of his sovereign purpose for the world.

Go about Zion, walk around her,
Count her towers, note her rampart,
Go through her strongholds (12–13a).

There could in fact be various reasons for such a tour of Jerusalem. Sennacherib made a survey like this to see what were the dimensions of the challenge which this city presented to his army: so Isaiah implies, as a preliminary to declaring that the man who counted the towers will soon disappear (Is. 33:18). Nehemiah surveyed the city to see what building was needed (Ne. 2). But the survey referred to in the psalm is more like the ones promised and described after these two events. Isaiah promised that they would be able to look on Jerusalem safe and whole and relieved of pressure (Is. 33:20). Nehemiah took the people in a procession of praise round the rebuilt walls, 'rejoicing with great joy' in what the Lord had done (Ne. 12). So the psalm envisages a tour which takes place after the bombing is over and the enemy has fled. 'Go and check' is its invitation. 'How has the city fared? You will find that every tower is still there, the walls are still intact, the fortifications have stood firm.' Perhaps the psalm indicates that the dramatic recalling of God's acts of salvation was followed up by a procession round the city of God, which again rejoiced to give him the glory for what he had done.

The purpose of it all, however, looked beyond the relieving of fears and the upbuilding of present faith. It is *so that you can recount to the generation to come* ... (13b). 'We have heard from our fathers' (*cf.* Ps. 44:1), the story has been handed on to us; now we have to pass it on to our children, as the torah exhorts us (*e.g.* Dt. 4:9–10). As we declare God's praise, we give glory to him and also bear witness to others—including people yet unborn.

Witness of what, however? 'So that you can recount to the generation to come that this is Zion, God's city'? On the contrary, the psalm is concerned with telling people about God, and it thus ends on the same note as it began, in praise not of the city of Zion but of the God of Zion. The purpose of the survey of Jerusalem is *so that you can recount to the generation to come that this is God, our God for all time; he will guide us for ever* (14).

Because the religion of the psalmist is ultimately centred not on a certain place but on a certain God, the place (though outwardly so crucial to the psalm) is not actually indispensable. The 'city of

God' is not so much local as personal, for the place of the presence of God, in Old and New Testaments, is not a location 'irrevocably fixed on a map; it depends on the Lord's will to be accessible to men . . . The place where the song is at home is where folk who know their identity in relation to the one named Yahweh form themselves in response to his presence'.[8] Zion does in fact become for the Jews themselves not a literal geographical location but an idea, a symbol, a hope. In a sense, of course, it had to, for this testimony to its being *the joy of the whole world* (verse 2) became completely empty with the exile. Any beauty it had was desecrated, and Lamentations puts on the lips of the heathen nations the question, 'Is this the city that was called "perfect beauty", "the joy of the whole world"?' (La. 2:15).

But even before the exile it had been realized that the Zion ideal, or the destiny of Zion, was bigger than the achieved reality even of the best times. The same is true, in fact, as is the case with the kingship. The idea is larger than life: thus Isaiah looks forward to a day when lowly Zion *will* be the highest of mountains (I imagine he is interested not in geological transformation but in its significance being manifest and acknowledged), when the nations will come to it not in attack but to seek the word of the Lord which will spread from here to the world (Is. 2:1–3).

As it happens, I am typing these words on Whit Sunday, and I cannot fail to note that on the first Christian Pentecost representatives of 'every nation under heaven' gathered in Jerusalem and witnessed the pouring out of God's Spirit (Acts 2:1–11); there they received the word of Christ, and from there that word was taken to the whole world. There is a form of historical fulfilment of the Zion vision. It is not the only possible one: a Jew today would probably want to point to the way the thinking of Israel (particularly its ethics) has more broadly influenced the whole of the civilization of the West.

In another sense again, the vision finds a further embodiment as the Holy Spirit of God comes to dwell in the midst of the people of Christ wherever they are and throughout their history. They of course still look forward to the heavenly Jerusalem, on its great high mountain, with its walls and gates and foundations (though without a temple, because the Lord is there in person:

[8] J. L. Mays, 'Worship, World, and Power: An Interpretation of Ps 100', *Interpretation* 23:3 (1969), p. 317.

Rev. 21). But at the same time they are even now actually already living in that Jerusalem. The dwelling of God is with man; he will dwell with them, and they will be his people.

What the New Testament says about the church is an ideal which, we have to confess, is only partially realized now—just as old Zion was an ideal. But there is at the same time now a real, though partial, experience of the presence of the power of God— an experience which whets our appetite for the fullness of the heavenly Jerusalem and also acts as a spur to entering now, as fully as is possible in this age, into the consummation of the age to come. A Christian has to live with an experience that will always fall short of this fullness, however. He remains a citizen of another city, only really at home on another mountain-top. And 'how can I sing Yahweh's song in a strange land?' (*cf*. Ps. 137:4). I can, because Yahweh is here with me, turning foreign soil into his dwelling-place. Thus here, too, I declare *Yahweh is great, and worthy of all praise* (Ps. 48:1).

GOD'S PEOPLE PUT IN THEIR PLACE (Psalm 50)

Yahweh Sabaoth is with us (46:7). We have noted above that this is a dangerous doctrine. The belief that God is with us, that he is committed to us willy-nilly, can lead to a neglect of the moral commitment that he demands: in Amos's day people said 'Yahweh Sabaoth is with us', but they were wrong, because they were not committed to good rather than evil (Am. 5:14). The belief that God is with us can lead to a false confidence that 'trouble will not come upon us', as it did in the time of Jeremiah (Je. 5:12). In the same period Zephaniah, too, talks of Yahweh as the one who is in the midst of the city and of the people: but he is concerned to drive home this message of the moral obligations of Yahweh's presence, for he is the God of righteousness and justice (Zp. 3:5). The centuries in which these prophets lived were not ones characterized by irreligion; there was much worship, much piety, of a sort. These prophets, however, demanded that the people of God forsake the besetting sin of trying to confine God to a box marked 'religion'; and in fact the misapprehension that God is interested in religion, not life, dies hard.

Psalm 50 exposes this fallacy. Like Psalm 47, it may well belong to the Festival of Tabernacles at the end of the year, when Israel recalled her redemption from Egypt, re-acknowledged Yahweh's Kingship over her, and (at least every sabbatical year) read through the covenant law and re-submitted herself to it (Dt. 31:9–13). So the psalm speaks of God coming to his covenant people (1–6), assessing their worship (7–15), and reminding them of where the heart of his demands lay (16–23).

The call of God (verses 1–6)

Two months after leaving Egypt, the Israelites encamped in Sinai. At a mountain there they were confronted by thunder and lightning, cloud and smoke, fire and earthquake (Ex. 19): all these are the accompaniments, or side-effects, of the appearing of God (whose actual appearance cannot be described). But they are also the antecedents to his speaking, for in the Bible, when God appears, he characteristically does so in order to speak. Theophany leads to theology, vision gives way to audition. This phenomenon is an important feature of Israelite religion; the phrase 'God spoke' is much more frequent in the Old Testament than the phrase 'God appeared'.

When the words came at Sinai, they concerned the terms of the relationship which was to obtain between Yahweh and the people he had begun to relate to. The matter is summed up at the opening of the story. 'You yourselves saw what I did to the Egyptians. I carried you on eagles' wings and brought you to myself. Now if you really listen to my voice and keep my covenant, you will be my most treasured possession among all the nations' (Ex. 19:4–5). The laws that follow itemize Yahweh's concerns and give content to the demand for obedience which he issues to his people, and Exodus further describes the mutual commitment sealed ceremonially at the foot of the mountain (Ex. 24:3–8), with heaven and earth later called to witness the obligations accepted by the people of God (Dt. 31:28; 32:1).

Yahweh, then, first thundered from Sinai. But then he took up his abode on another hill, outwardly much more humble, but given cosmic significance by his coming to dwell there. Thus the reverberations of Sinai's thunder and lightning, cloud and smoke, fire and earthquake are heard and felt as 'Yahweh roars from Zion and his voice thunders from Jerusalem' (Am. 1:2; *cf.* Pss. 97:1–5; 99:1–2). He thunders with judgment on the rebellious world; and the message is thus potentially a comforting one for his own people. Indeed it is intended to be so. They may rejoice that the heathen powers that oppose themselves to God and his people are to be put down.

The message easily becomes too comforting, however. The people of the world are to be judged not because of their status (that they do not belong to Israel) but because of their actions (they reject the Lordship of God). But the people of God, so-called, will also be judged, if they reject the Lordship of God. Their status (that they do belong to Israel) gives them no protection in this situation. For them, as Amos puts it, Yahweh's day of judgment will not be a day to greet with joy; it will have more the atmosphere of darkness and gloom (Am. 5:18-20).

Psalm 50 belongs against this background: that of Sinai and Zion, that of covenant and judgment. *The Mighty Lord, Yahweh,*[9] *has spoken. He has summoned the world, from east to west* (1). The opening words tell us that a judgment-scene is to be described, and the whole world is called to appear. *From Zion, the city of perfect beauty,*[1] *God's light has shone forth. Our God is coming, he is not keeping silence* (2-3a). He may have seemed negligent and inactive in the face of wickedness, but now he is coming, with those same cosmic audio-visual accompaniments that had manifested themselves at Sinai: *fire consumes before him, a storm rages around him. He summons heaven above, and the earth, to the judgment* (3b-4): the purpose of the gathering is now quite explicit. But there is a twist to the story. It is clear that heaven and earth are present not as the objects of judgment but as the witnesses of judgment, the role to which Deuteronomy calls them. *Let the heavens declare his justice, for God himself is giving judgment* (6). The knife twists as the psalmist declares that the object of judgment is not the world but the church. The gathering is one for the pronouncing of God's just judgment on his own people (4-5).[2] So he commands:

[9] More literally, 'El, God, Yahweh'. The relationship of the three words to each other is not clear (EVV offer various possibilities) but the general impression intended is one of majesty and power. El is the mighty one, the chief of the gods among the Canaanites; Yahweh is the sovereign, victorious 'Lord of Hosts'. God (*'elohim*) is the general word for deity, as in English. See also above, p. 76.

[1] The phrase picked up in Lamentations; see the comments at the end of the treatment of Ps. 48, above, p. 120.

[2] *Justice—ṣedeq*; giving judgment—*šōpēt*: on these two roots, see the comments on 48:10-11, above, pp. 117 f.

> Gather here those who committed themselves to me,[3]
> Those who made a covenant with me by sacrifice (5).

His people comprise *those who committed themselves*: that, at least, was their calling. They expressed their commitment, in the persons of their fathers, when the covenant was made back at Sinai (Ex. 24: 3–8), with the covenant's terrible implicit oath, 'May this (the tearing of the sacrificial animal into pieces) be done to me also, if I fail to keep the covenant I have made'.[4] But they have not kept their commitment and are summoned to the Lord's presence, not as witnesses of the judgment to be brought on others (as heaven and earth were), but to hear themselves declared guilty.

The people of God are ever in danger of relaxing, of assuming that they are all right. They see themselves as God's chosen, and they are that. But history is littered with people who let that conviction become a presumption. When God acts in judgment—whether at the end of time or in history—then judgment begins with the people of God (1 Pet. 4:17).

Religion in its place (verses 7–15)

Wherein lies the guilt of the people of God, however? For most of history, man has been incurably religious. He has produced all sorts of theological frameworks for his religion, and all sorts of liturgical expressions of it. But the same religious instinct underlies all these.

The New Testament explicitly repudiates religion. God is not located on a particular mountain, but wherever people gather in Christ's name (Jn. 4:21; Mt. 18:20). The sacrifices God looks for are not the offering of dead animals but the presenting of the living self to God (Rom. 12:1). The church has argued on and on about the right performance of its cult (what makes a valid eucharist? where should the minister stand?), has dignified its buildings by the title 'house of God' when the phrase belongs

---

[3] *ḥªsîḏāw*, the adjective/noun connected with *ḥeseḏ* which was discussed on page 32, in connection with 43:1. As is noted there, Hasidim becomes (and still is) a title for the especially orthodox Jews. But in this passage, at least, it denotes the position and calling of the people as a whole.

[4] *Made a covenant* is literally 'cut a covenant'; the phrase probably recalls a ceremony such as that described in Gn. 15.

only to the congregation that meets there, and has centred its concerns on affairs of piety—and ignored the Bible's priorities.

The struggle with religion goes back behind the New Testament into the Old. Of course the laws provide regulations for worship, indicating what manner of religion Yahweh approves of. But is it insignificant that the first religious offerings of all were brought not by God's will but by man's, and that they are the cause of the first envy, strife and murder (Gn. 4)? Evidently sacrifice was not God's idea; it was an expression of what men thought he would like. And characteristically God starts where men are. He accepts one of the offerings, he uses the human religious instinct, he gives regulations for it, he turns it into a means of picturing what the healing of relationships between him and man must and will involve. But religion is put in its place.

It is difficult for the people of God to accept the low place he gives to religion, however; they are inclined to assume that he cannot have enough of their offerings. It is this misapprehension that the psalmist deals with first (7–15), before going on to remind them of where his real interests lie (16–22).

> *Listen, my people, and I will speak.*
> *Listen, Israel, and I will bear witness against you:*
> *I am God, your God.*
> *For your offerings*[5] *I do not rebuke you,*
> *Nor for your whole offerings,*[6] *always before me* (7–8).

Both these major forms of ritual, the communion offerings and the whole burnt offerings, involved real 'sacrifice' on the part of the worshippers. And Israel had not failed to make the sacrifice,

---

[5] The word used here, *zebāḥîm*, is a general one, like the corresponding English one, but it is often used to refer to a particular group of sacrifices, namely those which the offerer shared in eating (they are consequently sometimes referred to as communion offerings). Since the *whole offerings*, mentioned next, were ones of which the offerer ate nothing, it is probably the case that the communion offerings are meant in this line. Lv. 7 refers to three occasions on which they might be offered: by way of thanksgiving (verses 12–15), in response to Yahweh's goodness; as freewill offerings (16–17), offered out of devotion, not obligation; and in fulfilment of a vow made in prayer (16–17). See de Vaux, pp. 417 f.

[6] Offerings which were entirely burnt, as a sign that they were given wholly to God, to whom their smoke ascended as a 'pleasing fragrance' (Gn. 8:21).

to 'waste' their possessions for God's sake. He has no complaints in this area.

> *I would not take a bull from your home*
> *Or a goat from your folds* (9).

He has no need to, of course, because he already possesses all that lives on the earth:

> *For to me belongs every creature of the forest,*
> *The cattle on the hills by the thousand.*
> *I know every bird on the hills,*[7]
> *Everything that moves in the countryside is in my care.*
> *If I get hungry,*[8] *I would not tell you—*
> *The world and all it contains are mine* (10–12).

But of course the whole idea of God being hungry, and needing their offerings lest he should starve, is nonsense:

> *Do I eat beef*
> *And drink goats' blood?* (13).

It seems likely that, according to primitive ideas, the point about sacrifice was to feed the god. It is doubtful whether this idea was ever accepted in Israel at an official level (otherwise, presumably, the laws would allocate a better cut of the meat to God than they in fact do!). But the Israelites' apparent desire to make huge offerings to God almost suggested that this was the way they thought.

No. Sacrifice is just an outward expression of the 'please' and 'thank you' of a personal relationship.

> *Make a thankoffering to God,*[9]
> *Fulfil your vows to the Most High.*

[7] One cannot but recall Mt. 10:29.

[8] The irony is heavy here, since the psalmist speaks as if there were actually a possibility of God getting hungry.

[9] JB, TEV, RSVmg. interpret this as an exhortation to non-sacrificial worship, but this is not at all the natural way to take the words, especially in a context full of references to sacrifice. What the psalmist is demanding is not the abandonment of sacrifice but the abandonment of an implied misunderstanding of it.

Call on me in time of trouble;
I will rescue you, and you will give me glory (14–15).

Here is a vignette of the life of prayer and promise, response and praise, which is how God wishes his people would live. His people call on him in trouble, and part of the motivation of their prayer is the commitment to giving him the glory when he answers. Clearly this could become a mere pragmatic business arrangement between man and God, but it need not be that. They can make these vows out of real devotion, and he can accept them with fatherly joy. Further, with fatherly joy he responds to their prayer and rescues them; then he thrills to watch them come back to his house to bring the praise they promised and to express their joy in the outward thankoffering.

In fact, the thrust of this section of the psalm is to exclude the notion that the worship of the temple is a business affair. If it were, then the bigger the sacrifice, the bigger the answer to prayer. But biblical faith does not work that way. The very simplicity of outward worship draws attention to the fact that the real business, the real relationship, is the one you cannot see. The challenge of this section of the psalm is to examine the nature of our relationship with God to see whether we are living with him the life of prayer and promise, response and testimony, which the psalmist takes as the heart of true religion.

Where real failure lies (verses 16–23)

The psalm began by declaring that God had a case to bring: against his own people. It went on to eliminate one area where they might have thought they needed to do more. The final section makes clear where God's real interest, and his real indictment, lie. It links further with the opening section, in that there the psalmist recalled the making of the covenant (verse 5) and the declaration with which the covenant commandments begin: *I am Yahweh your God* (Ex. 20:2; *cf.* verse 7).[1] The recollection is a pointed one, for, as the last section of the psalm reminds the worshippers, they are in breach of those covenant requirements. Theft and adultery are proscribed by the commandments but

---

[1] Presumably *I am Yahweh your God* was the phrase which originally appeared in verse 7 (see on 42:8, above, pp. 37 ff.), though admittedly in the Hebrew the words are in a different order from the version in the decalogue.

practised in Israel, and even if the hearers are not personally involved, they are tolerant of these matters:

> *Whenever you see a thief, you connive with him;*
> *You associate with adulterers* (18).

The very first psalm warns against such one-step-removed involvement with evil: it is antithetical to delighting in God's word and being sustained by him (Ps. 1:1–3).

Other psalms which stress God's moral demands of those who come to worship him emphasize sins of the tongue (15:1–3; 24:3–4), also proscribed by the commandments (Ex. 20:16). So, in Psalm 50, alongside permissiveness is set deceit:

> *You dedicate your mouth to evil,*
> *You harness your tongue to deceit* (19).

The psalmist devises two very vivid expressions to indict the cheating of one's neighbour of what belongs to him. Then alongside deceit is set slander, which may be another way of cheating others of what is rightfully theirs:

> *You sit speaking against your brother,*
> *You slander your own mother's son* (20).

It may be that at each point those who were being accused here would have been surprised. They personally avoided theft and adultery. They were not involved in robbery and violence. But the psalmist sees permissiveness and sharp business practice as no better. It is tantamount to despising and abandoning Yahweh's word.

> *You . . . refuse my instruction*
> *And throw off my words*[2] (17).

Consequently, it is highly incongruous for Israel to stand as a congregation before the Lord and profess to accept the covenant based on these words. It is just nonsense:

[2] Not his words in general, probably, but his commands (*cf*. Ex. 20:1). The decalogue is spoken of as the ten 'words' (*e.g.* Ex. 34:28).

> *What are you doing reciting my laws*
> *And speaking of my covenant?* (16).

And God will not ignore the affront.

> *These are the things you have done: could I remain silent?*
> *You have planned people's ruin*[3] *: could I be like you?* (21).

So, having called the world to the judgment-scene, God testifies against his people (*cf.* verse 7). He is not like them, uncaring about evil:

> *I will charge you, I will set out my case before you* (21c).

The covenant offered Israel the choice between life and death, blessing and curse, and in this situation where Israel is on trial before Yahweh a similar choice is set before her. We have recalled already how Amos spoke of the Lord roaring like a lion (Am. 1:2). It is no empty roar. He will go on to treat them the way a lion does his helpless prey.

> *Won't you see this, you who leave God out of account?*
> *Otherwise I will tear you to pieces, and there will be no-one to rescue*
> *you*[4] (22).

More literally, the hearers are spoken of as 'you who forget God'. But we have seen already that, in Hebrew, forgetting, like remembering and knowing, is not thought of as an involuntary mental process, but as an act of the will with practical consequences. To remember is to bring to mind, to take account of, and to do something about; to know is to recognize, to acknowledge; to forget is to put out of one's mind, to ignore, to abandon. Forgetting is a wilful, moral act, and is judged as such.

There is the way of death, of the curse. The way of blessing, the way of life, is the simple way of faith, with the two aspects which the psalm as a whole presupposes. One is the life of worship: *The man who brings a thankoffering*[5] *honours me* (23a). The other

---

[3] *Cf.* Dahood, except that I take *ḥayyôṭ* to mean destruction, calamity (*cf.* Jb. 6:2; Ps. 52:4).

[4] The description is applied explicitly to the attack of a lion in 7:2.

[5] It is unlikely that the reference is to spiritual sacrifice (*cf.* RSV, JB, TEV); see on verses 14–15, above.

is the life of moral obedience: *To the man who orders his way, I will show the salvation of God* (23b).

There, indeed, are the two outward expressions of the life of faith. The church has often lost one or other of them. On the one hand, when it becomes entrapped in religion it misses the way of God. It has often done this: very obviously in unreformed catholicism, but also in protestantism. Protestants, too, can fall into the trap of thinking that the thing that God is really interested in is their prayer meetings and their fellowship hours; these can be a way of avoiding the demands of his will. On the other side, Christians have often fallen short of the moral demands of God. It is easy to be incredulous over the moral blindspots of a previous generation (how could Christians have acquiesced so long in the oppression of black peoples?) without allowing for the possibility that future centuries will be equally astonished at what we cannot see about ourselves. A clergyman recently expressed the opinion to me that Christian congregations could hardly be in need of the kind of upbraiding that the prophets give to Israel in her obstinacy. I am not so confident that the substantial obedience of the people of God can be assumed. Rather we need to stand under the judgment that a psalm such as this one brings to the congregation of the Lord, and ask earnestly and openly, 'Lord, is it I? Lord, do we take our status for granted? Lord, do we try to fob you off with our piety? Lord, where are our moral blindspots?' The demands that God lays upon his people are simple to understand and simple to evade.

But God will ransom ...
(Psalm 49)

The choirmaster's.   The Korahites'.   A psalm.

1 *Listen to this, all you peoples.*
  Give heed, all who live on the earth,
2 *All men and everyone, rich and poor alike.*
3 *My mouth will speak true wisdom,*
  My heart will express its insight.
4 *I will bend my ear to instruction,*
  I will resolve my problem in my music.

5 *Why should I be afraid in bad days,*
  When perverseness and deceit surround me,
6 *People who trust in their assets,*
  Who glory in the vastness of their riches?
7 *It is impossible for a person to ransom his brother.*
  He could not pay God his price.
8 *The ransom for their life would be too great,*
  It would never be completed,
9 *That he should live on for ever,*
  Not see the Pit.
10 *No. He will see that wise men die,*
   The foolish and stupid alike perish:
   They leave their assets to others.
11 *Their tomb is their home for ever,*
   Their dwelling for all time.
   They name the earth as their own.

12   *Despite his prestige, man's life does not last.*
      He is one with the cattle doomed to slaughter.

13 *This is what happens to them, with all their confidence,*
    And their followers who accept their words.   Pause

14 *They are put like sheep in Sheol;*
    Death shepherds them.
    The upright have dominion over them at the Morning.
    Their bodies are to be wasted by Sheol,
    A magnificent house for them.

15 *But God will ransom my life.*
    He will surely take me from the power of Sheol.   Pause

16 *Do not be afraid when a man becomes rich,*
    When the honour of his family grows,

17 *For he will take nothing with him when he dies.*
    His honour does not go down with him.

18 *He indeed blesses himself as long as he lives—*
    'People acknowledge that you have done well for yourself'.

19 *He goes to join his ancestors,*
    Who will never again see the light.

20   *Man with prestige but without insight*
      Is one with the cattle doomed to slaughter.

Death is today the great unmentionable, as sex was for the Victorians. Actually this has been said so often, it can no longer be true: hardly a month passes without television or the heavyweight Sunday newspapers philosophizing on the subject, or discussing the merits of cheap funerals, or relating the testimony of the about-to-die or the recently bereaved. Yet (as with sex, in fact) much talking may have the same significance as silence: it is an indication that the subject is still a problem. The demon still needs exorcizing; bringing the matter out into the open and talking about it is a way of doing that.

Because the Psalms are concerned with life, they cannot but be concerned with death also—for there can be no satisfying understanding of the meaning of life which has not grappled with the meaning of death. Psalm 49 approaches the question from a particular theological perspective (one not otherwise widely represented in the Psalter), that of the Wisdom tradition in Israel. Like Proverbs, it speaks of *wisdom* and *insight* (3), of a *proverb* and a *riddle* (4, RSV), of the fate of the *wise*, the *foolish*, and the *stupid*

(10). Like Job and Ecclesiastes, it takes up basic questions about the meaning of human life in the context of experiences which suggest that in reality there is no meaning.

The distinctiveness of the Wisdom tradition is that it takes up these questions without overtly presupposing Israel's special relationship with God. The historians and prophets and priests of the Old Testament assume that there is a particularly close relationship between Yahweh and Israel, expressed in her history and her worship. This belief adds a new dimension to the meaning of life, and makes it easier to cope with experiences that suggest that there is no meaning; these experiences are put in perspective by the fact that Yahweh has certainly made himself known in Israel's history and worship.[1] The Christian approaches life on a similar basis as he sees his experience of life within the further context of the coming of Christ and the giving of the Spirit.

But the Wisdom tradition, for whatever reason, seems not to presuppose such a perspective. The Wisdom books do not refer to Yahweh's promises and their fulfilment, to the covenant and the temple, to the Messiah and the Day of the Lord. They are concerned with how everyday life actually works. Their starting-point, it might be said, is general revelation (God's making himself known in various ways to men everywhere) rather than special revelation (God's revealing himself through particular events and people). Part of their value is precisely their determination to take this approach as far as it can be taken, but part also is their unveiling of where that boundary lies, as we shall see below.

So how does the wise psalmist understand death?

WHAT DEATH TERMINATES

Christianity has sometimes been 'world-denying' and taken a negative attitude to the things of this life. Indeed, in reminding hedonistic ages of the limited value of this life's achievements and enjoyments (as Ecclesiastes does), it has performed the world a useful service.

The Bible, however, is markedly 'world-affirming'. It delights

[1] Cf. J. Bowker, Problems of Suffering in Religions of the World (Cambridge University Press, 1970), pp. 5–9.

in life, in creation, in man and woman, in the laughter of children and the achievement of maturity. The Son of man himself was classically accused of enjoying life too much (Mt. 11:19). The psalmist praises God not only for bread but for strong drink and (male) make-up (Ps. 104:15). It all goes back to creation and to God's declaration that the world was 'good'—even 'beautiful'.

Thus part of the significance of death is that so much that is good is now lost.

The light of life extinguished

The secret of living on *for ever* (9) has fascinated story-teller and scientist. The so-called Babylonian flood story, the Gilgamesh Epic, is about a man searching for immortality—but he never finds it. A science-fiction poem describes a man whose brain was fixed in chemical when he died, so that he could carry on—the scientists are not sure what he can carry on doing, but something is still happening, he still exists.[2] A recent 'Doctor Who' series manifested the same motif—and, indeed, the 'Time Lords' themselves embody this human aspiration.

The Old Testament itself pictures man as given God's life but then agonizingly forbidden to eat of the tree of life and thus live for ever (Gn. 2:7; 3:22). It sees human life as God's gift which expresses something of his own nature—for he is 'the living God', he is alive and active on man's behalf (*cf.* Jos. 3:10; Ps. 18:46[3]). Life implies liveliness, aliveness, vitality, activity. For man it is a gift received from God, and enjoyed by faith in and commitment to God (Hab. 2:4; Am. 5:4, 14).

> 'You show me the path that leads to life;
> there is joy which satisfies in your presence,
> there are delights for ever at your right hand' (Ps. 16:11).

Thus 'life' means 'enjoyment both of real goods regarded as the blessing of Yahweh on the one hand and of living fellowship with God, whose unshakeable certainty gives joy to the righteous, on the other'.[4]

[2] 'Tithonus' by D. M. Thomas in *Penguin Modern Poets* 11: D. M. Black, Peter Redgrove, D. M. Thomas (Pelican Books, 1969), pp. 99–103.

[3] Also Ps. 42:2; see the comments, above, on this passage, pp. 28 ff.

[4] G. von Rad, 'Life and Death in the Old Testament', *TDNT* II, p. 845.

Closely associated with life is light. 'With you is the fountain of life; by your light we see light' (Ps. 36:9). And as 'life' suggests 'fullness of life' (not mere existence), so 'light' suggests not merely 'sight' but 'insight' and awareness of God. 'Yahweh is my light and my salvation ... Yahweh is the fortress of my life' (Ps. 27:1, JB): 'light', 'life' and 'salvation' are bound up together.

But death terminates life and light. In the moment of dying the eyes close. As Psalm 49 itself puts it, one will not *live on for ever* (9); one *will never again see the light* (19).

You can't take it with you

Prosperity, too, is a gift from God. Wheat and barley, iron and copper, food and homes, herds and flocks, silver and gold—these are among God's blessings (Dt. 8:7–13). Not that some are meant to have these to excess and others to be poor; God wants all his creatures to enjoy the good things he has created. Nor that wrong attitudes cannot be taken to them—as indeed to spiritual blessings. God warns his people not to let his blessings beguile them away from him (Dt. 8:11–20), and the men of whom the psalmist speaks had fallen into some such trap as this. Although he refers to 'the wickedness of treacherous foes' (5, NEB[5]), the affliction of the weak by the strong is not his central concern. He speaks much more of the wrong attitudes to wealth which their prosperity leads them to.

What is this prosperity? To start at the material level, it is *riches* (6b; *cf. rich* in 2, 16a): wealth, possessions, 'things'. Israel in Old Testament times was not primarily a monetary economy, and riches would mean lands and buildings (*cf.* Is. 5:8; Am. 5:11) and other such solid, visible assets, not subject to the erosion of inflation and clearly worth possessing.

But once you get beyond what you can use yourself, what is significant about possessions (as is the case with money) is what you can do with them. They are resources or *assets* (6a, 10).[6] They

---

[5] Perhaps even this implies more active hostility than the words actually mean to suggest; *cf.* the discussion of the verse, below, p. 141.

[6] The word *ḥayil* (*wealth* or *riches* in EVV) most often means 'army', but also 'strength' and 'personal ability/worth/qualities', as well as 'wealth'. If there is a common thread running through these varied notions, it may be that of 'resources'—military, physical, personal/psychological, financial; the means whereby to effect what needs to be done in various connections. BDB gives 'strength' as the word's basic idea.

open up all sorts of possibilities before you. Money talks. It brings you *prestige* (12, 20).[7] It is inevitable and not inappropriate that prosperity is recognized and honoured. Related to this acknowledgement is the further gain of status or *honour* (16, 17).[8] The wealthy are generally in practice the 'upper class'; 'riches' implies 'honour'. And the man who finds these good things *indeed blesses himself as long as he lives*—'*People acknowledge*[9] *that you have done well for yourself*' (18).

Riches, assets, prestige, honour, the sense of achievement, recognition: all are fine. But they are transitory. For all a man's riches in this life, *he will take nothing with him when he dies* (17a). Whoever men are, death means that *they leave their assets to others* (10c): they cannot realize their potential, others will do so instead. Death means that *despite his prestige, man's life does not last* (12a)—more literally, he *does not abide*; for, as the New Testament puts it, only faith, hope and love 'abide' (1 Cor. 13:13)—prestige does not. Death means that a man's *honour* dissolves; it *does not go down with him* to Sheol (17b). Death means that all a man's achievement and recognition are short-lived, and he ends up where everyone else does: *he goes to join his ancestors, who will never again see the light* (19).

In 1975 the BBC networked a programme of regional origin about how a young man and his family in Lancashire faced up to the fact that he was discovered to have only a few weeks to live. The programme was called 'Remember the Good Things'. That was all there was to do. They had been good, but with death they were over.

[7] The word *yᵉqār* usually suggests the idea of being valuable or valued, and thus honoured because one's value is recognized. The word is not pejorative (as RSV *pomp* might imply).

[8] The regular word for the *glory* of God (*kābôd*) as well as for the *honour* of man. It is sometimes translated simply 'wealth' (so NEB here), but carries the overtone of the respected position that wealth brings.

[9] This verb (*y-d-h*) is the one often translated 'praise' or 'thank' when God is the object (*e.g.* Pss. 42:5, 11; 43:4, 5; 44:8). But the fact that it can be used of the recognition of facts suggests that the basic idea of this word, even when used of man's attitude to God, is not that I *feel* full of praise or thanks (as words such as 'I am grateful' suggest in English), nor that I make a joyful noise in praise (as the other common Hebrew word *h-l-l*—as in 'hallelujah'— does suggest). Both these ideas are valid ones, though they may have the danger of drawing attention to *my* feelings and *my* words; *y-d-h* directs all attention away from me to the God whom I acknowledge. *Cf.* Westermann, pp. 25–33.

It is difficult for people to accept that this is the case. When someone loses their husband or wife, they commonly carry on dreaming about them, even seeing them. It is difficult to accept that they are really gone. But they are. The psalmist wants his contemporaries not to be beguiled into behaving as if the good things of which he speaks are eternal. The time will come when they are gone. The Bible's classic illustration of this is Jesus' story about the rich man who died suddenly when he thought he was set up for life. His blindness to this possibility has earned him an immortality of a kind—he is remembered as the rich *fool* (Lk. 12:16–21). The man whose treasure is his riches, his resources, his prestige, his status, his sense of achievement, his recognition, loses all these when he dies. What are they replaced by?

WHAT DEATH BRINGS

Man is a perplexing combination. He was made in God's image and commissioned to govern the created world (Gn. 1:27–28). A distinctiveness of man over against (other) animals, though difficult to define, is presupposed. And yet *he is one with the cattle doomed to slaughter* (12b, 20b, JB).

'The same fate awaits man and animal alike. One dies just like the other. They are both the same kind of creature. A human being is no better off than an animal, because life has no meaning for either. They are both going to the same place—the dust. They both came from it; they will both go back to it' (Ec. 3:19–20, TEV).

Of course one difference about human beings has been their concern with burial. They do not generally just abandon the dead, but seek to give them a permanent resting-place. But what a place to lie in state: *their tomb is their home for ever* (the phrase 'an eternal home' is the kind of euphemism beloved by undertakers; *cf.* Ec. 12:5); *their dwelling for all time* (11)!

So man ends up where he started; he returns to the ground from which he was taken (Gn. 3:19; *cf.* the quotation from Ecclesiastes above). The point is made specifically here at the end of verse 11: when men die, *they name* (acknowledge) *the earth as their own.*[1] At his death and burial *'āḏām* (man) acknowledges that he is *'ᵃḏāmāh* (earth).

The point is made again ironically at the end of verse 14: Sheol will be *a magnificent house*[2] *for them.* The word used here suggests a place of honour and exaltation, 'a glorious habitation' (Is. 63:15), 'an exalted house' (1 Ki. 8:13), a place to lie in state indeed. But the euphemism is heavy with irony, for it is the place where *their bodies are to be wasted by Sheol* (14). It is, to put it more crudely, simply *the Pit* (9). The expression reflects a burial custom. A family's ideal would be to own its own family tomb, where succeeding generations would be buried. To die was to join one's ancestors (19a) in a very down-to-earth sense: the tomb's stone door would be moved, the new body would be placed on one of the ledges in the man-made or natural cave, and then the door would be replaced. Darkness would return to the cavern, and except for the periodic repetition of these sad and brief moments you and your ancestors would *never again see the light* (19b). But not everyone could be buried in such a family tomb, and there were also common graves (*cf.* Je. 26:23), sometimes a communal grave pit; and it is presumably this practice that lies behind the reference to seeing *the Pit.*

But the references to Sheol and to the Pit and to being with one's ancestors of course suggest more than the physical fate of the body in the grave. The body is the solid and visible expression of the person as a whole; its experience reflects that of the whole person. While it would be an exaggeration to say that the Old Testament does not distinguish soul and body, it certainly does not make the sharp disjunction between them which characterized Platonic thought and has influenced popular Christian assumptions. The soul is not the true person which can happily survive the loss of the body ('John Brown's body lies a-mouldering in the grave, but his soul is marching on'), perhaps even regarding this loss as the shedding of an encumbrance. The physical person is the em-bodi-ment, the incarnation, of the true self, and is essential to the true self. In fact a man is lost without a body to 'clothe' his self (*cf.* 2 Cor. 5:4). So what happens to the body is an outward expression of what happens to the person; when the body dies and joins one's ancestors' remains in the

[1] *Cf.* van der Ploeg.
[2] *Cf.* van der Ploeg.

tomb, this is the outward expression of what happens to the self. The whole person loses its liveliness, its vitality. The languid inner man joins others in Sheol, the invisible equivalent to the physical pit or grave, the realm of the dead beneath the earth (*cf.* Nu. 16:30–33), 'behind' where the physical bodies were put.

Psalm 49 describes man's coming to Sheol by means of a grim re-application of a familiar Old Testament image. God is his people's shepherd, they are his sheep (*cf.* Ps. 23; Is. 40:11; Ezk. 34). But at death they are shepherded elsewhere by another hand: *they are put like sheep in Sheol; Death shepherds them* (14). No longer God, but Death is my shepherd. Death is quite often personified in Old Testament poetry (*e.g.* Je. 9:21; Ho. 13:14), and in the New Testament also (*cf.* 1 Cor. 15:26, 55). In other ancient Near Eastern religions Death is one of the gods; it is pictured as a greedy monster swallowing whomever it can (*cf.* Hab. 2:5). This may be the idea here in Psalm 49 too—*Death feeds on them* (*cf.* 14, AV) instead of feeding them (*cf.* Ezk. 34:1–10); Death shepherds people to what turns out to be a slaughterhouse.

Sheol means relief from the pressures and demands of life (Jb. 3:17–19), but it is the rest of inactivity, in a land of gloom and darkness. Here God is absent and unmindful, unpraised and unremembered (Pss. 6:5; 88:5, 10–12; Is. 38:18). He is, of course, in ultimate control here too; Sheol is naked before him (Jb. 26:6) and he can reach into Sheol as he wills (Ps. 139:8; Am. 9:2), especially to rescue those whom Sheol seeks to claim undeserved before their time (Pss. 16:10; 30:3; 86:13; Jon. 2:2). But their time comes eventually for all: even those who refused to face up to its inexorable demand. And then *the upright have dominion over them at the Morning*[3] (14). When the Day of the Lord dawns, the positions of the righteous and the wicked will be reversed—the latter will no longer be lord over the former. In the meantime, however, and until that Day dawns, Sheol is the lot of all men. The destiny of the body and of the inner man, the real self, is death, the grave, Sheol.

[3] So MT, which is quite intelligible (despite NEB mg.), but which may not be original. The idea of the positions of the righteous and the wicked being reversed at the day of judgment belongs to the latest Old Testament period, and the psalm does not otherwise refer to final judgment. Thus RSV and others assume that slight (but far-reaching) alterations have been made in the text to produce MT. *Cf. BHS.*

What difference does Christianity make to this pre-Christian way of thinking? The beginnings of a distinction between the good and evil destiny after death of righteous and unrighteous appear in the Old Testament period (*e.g.* Ps. 73), and this very psalmist looks to an experience of Yahweh rescuing him from a meaningless end to life (15). Daniel 12 offers the only undisputed Old Testament reference to resurrection;[4] both this passage and Psalm 49 show how the development of this hope stemmed from an increasing awareness that justice is not done in this life, that the righteous suffer and the unrighteous prosper.[5] God's love, God's faithfulness, God's righteousness *will* operate on behalf of his true people.

This is the Old Testament's developing hope. But it could become reality only through Christ. In a real sense death had every right to claim the lives even of the relatively righteous of the people of God; for they were only relatively righteous, and thus (compared with God's own standard) relatively unrighteous and appropriately barred from access to the tree of life (Gn. 3:24). Thus even the 'saints' of Old Testament times went to Sheol, for Christ's death and resurrection alone open Sheol (*cf.* Mt. 27:52–53). They will do that in a final sense only at the End, at the final resurrection. In the meantime, even after Christ, the time after one's death and before this resurrection is a time of non-fulfilment. We are, of course, secure, we are with Christ (Phil. 1:23). But we are not yet fully alive, not yet complete; we still look forward to that resurrection.

At least we have that hope. But it is a hope only for those in Christ. Apart from Christ, death replaces all the good things of life by the tomb as a home, by a return to the dust, by a descent to the Pit, by the shepherding of Sheol, by the wasting of the body, by the darkness of the grave. What consequences does this bring? Is there any way out?

[4] Passages such as Ho. 6:2 and Ezk. 37 refer to the 'rebirth' of the nation rather than the resurrection of individuals; so in my opinion does Is. 26:19, though this verse is often taken as a promise of the resurrection of individuals.

[5] Job's reaching out for vindication after death (*e.g.* 19:23–27) also begins from the fact that he does not receive vindication now.

SOME BLIND ALLEYS

If this is the perspective within which human life must be approached, how may a man face the future? The psalmist alludes to several assumptions about life which men often make, but which a realistic facing-up to the future will disallow.

Might is right?

The starting-point of the psalmist's wrestling with God and with truth is the fact that sometimes everything seems to go wrong and life seems nothing but a disaster. On these *bad days*[6] I may feel that *perverseness and deceit*[7] *surround me* (5). But, the psalm asserts, a realization that the 'might is right' approach to life leads to a death from which there is no rescue casts doubt on whether, as an approach to life, it is the last word.

Money talks?

We have noted, however, that the psalmist's real concern is with his foes' assumptions about wealth. They *trust in their assets* and *glory in the vastness of their riches* (6). These seem to constitute the key to an abundant life.

But the verbs that the psalmist uses are revealing. Grammatically the sentence is fine, but theologically it is grotesque; for these verbs 'to trust' and 'to glory' are designed to be used with God as their object. I have done wrong, Job acknowledges,

'if I have put my confidence in gold,
or declared my trust in fine gold;
if I have exulted in the vastness of my resources,
or in the abundance I have come to possess' (Jb. 31:24-25).

On the contrary, Jeremiah exhorts,

'The wise man is not to glory in his wisdom,
the hero is not to glory in his heroism,

---

[6] *ra^c* includes not only what is (morally) evil but what is experienced as distressful and calamitous. It is evil in the sense of calamity that God is said to be the creator of—not moral evil (Is. 45:7). BDB (p. 948b) takes this as the meaning here; *cf.* Pss. 23:4; 94:13.

[7] Literally 'the perverseness of my deceivers'.

> the rich man is not to glory in his riches;
> the man who glories is to glory in this,
> that he understands and knows me' (Je. 9:23–24).

Not that the psalmist had been in a position to be superior. His problem was fear (5). Probably he refers not merely to a fear of what the rich and wicked might do to him. The fear he speaks of[8] is more generalized than that. Their prosperity, their power, their doing well despite their godlessness, threaten his whole view of life and of God.[9] Is there no justice? He fears there may not be. And his anxiety puts him in no position to be superior in relation to the godless, because the verb 'to fear', too, is designed to be used with God as its object. 'Yahweh watches over those who fear him . . . he delivers them from death' (Ps. 33:18–19): precisely in the face of death fear, trust and pride are misplaced if they are directed to man. That is atheism.

After all, earthly riches cannot in fact protect from death, as the attitude of the wealthy to them seemed to presuppose. The realization of all earthly assets could not meet the ransom-price that would enable a man to live on for ever (7–9).

Now there were certain situations in which God would accept a 'ransom' instead of the life due to him. The life of the first-born was owed to him, for instance, as a sign that his Lordship over all was acknowledged (Ex. 13:2, 11–12). But human first-born were not to be actually sacrificed, they were to be ransomed (Ex. 13:13–15). God's claim on them was thus acknowledged, but they themselves could live. But such an arrangement could be made only if the party to whom the obligation was due allowed it. And there is no such ransom arrangement at the end of a life. Then *it is impossible for a person to ransom his brother*[1] (7). The words recall God's instructions to Noah, which speak of *a man* being responsible for taking the life of *his brother* (*i.e.* his fellow human being) if he commits murder (Gn. 9:6). The punishment for murder cannot be commuted to a fine (Nu. 35:31); wealth cannot

---

[8] See further, verse 16, where he urges others not to make his mistake.

[9] There is another parallel with the book of Job. Job's problem is not merely his suffering: it is that his present experience threatens to make nonsense of his understanding of God and man.

[1] *Brother* ('*āḥ*) comes first in the Hebrew, which is odd; some MSS read '*ak*, and EVV follow (*e.g.* RSV *truly*). But the parallel with Gn. 9:6 is striking and '*ak* looks like a correction of '*āḥ*.

buy a man off when he is guilty. *He could not pay God his price. The ransom for their life would be too great* (7–8). Here the words recall the law that regulated when a ransom-price could in fact be paid, that is in cases of accidental homicide, when a man by negligence causes the death of another: 'if a price is put on him, he shall pay the ransom for his life' (Ex. 21:30). The reference at the same time recalls the possibility of ransom in certain situations, and also declares that this is not one of those situations.[2] God's hypothetical price is too high, *it would never be completed, that he should live for ever, not see the Pit* (8–9). You just cannot rescue from God's hands a man who is destined for death. Through this life money talks. But at the end its bid falls on deaf ears.

Use your mind?

The psalm is a 'wisdom psalm'. It is the work of an intellectual, of a philosopher. The author wants there to be understanding and insight (3). But he is wise enough, and honest enough, to acknowledge the limitations of wisdom.

> *Wise men die;*
> *The foolish and stupid alike perish* (10).

In some situations wisdom is infinitely preferable to folly. But here the psalmist plumbs its ultimate inadequacy. He does not merely voice the awareness that the wisdom that man can achieve has limitations when it is judged by some ultimate standard, despite its admitted usefulness. He actually asserts that it is of no more use than ignorance. Once again, Ecclesiastes has said the last word on the matter: 'Oh, I know, "Wisdom is better than foolishness, just as light is better than darkness. Wise men can see where they are going, and fools cannot." But I also know that the same fate is waiting for us all. I thought to myself, "I will suffer the same fate as fools. So what have I gained from being so wise?" "Nothing," I answered, "not a thing." ... We must all die—wise and foolish alike' (Ec. 2:13–16, TEV). Philosophy is in the end of the day only a game. It has no answer in the face of death.

[2] Similar words occur also in Jb. 33:19–28, where Elihu offers the interesting speculation that an angel might represent a sick man to God and declare that he has found a ransom for him—what the ransom is is not made explicit.

Shut your eyes, and hope for the best?

Although the psalmist sees the limitations of philosophy, he does not praise the fool. On the contrary, he derides the fool's *confidence* (13). It is another word which can be used in a good sense, of trust placed in God: 'Yahweh will be your confidence' (Pr. 3:26; *cf.* Ps. 78:7). But it is more often the description of a false trust, as here: *foolish confidence* (RSV), *self-assurance* (JB). This 'fool'[3] is one incapable of concentration (Pr. 17:24), or reflection (17:16), or learning (15:14), or restraint (14:16), or self-knowledge (14:8); one who opens his mouth only to change feet (26:7, 9), who prefers opening his mouth to opening his ears (18:2) and comfortable illusions to truth (17:10); who *will* not see sense (23:9). But his devil-may-care bravado brings no exemption from death. Rather it takes him there: *this is what happens to them, with all their confidence . . . They are put like sheep in Sheol* (13a, 14a).

The fool, then, makes an inadvisable guide (Pr. 13:20). But, alas, although he 'gives himself away as soon as he opens his mouth',[4] with his big talk he is adept at taking others with him: *their followers who accept their words*[5] (13b) share their fate. Their gullibility leads them to accept the advice, admonition and invitations of the fool with his big mouth. But 'a fool's mouth is his destruction' (Pr. 18:7); 'his confidence is only a thread, his assurance a spider's web' (Jb. 8:14). And his very confidence, false and wilfully foolish as it is, is one reason why he has to fall.

So the psalmist cuts the ground from under four ways of living with life. The reality of death confutes the arrogance of power, the security of wealth, the wisdom of the philosopher and the bravado of the fool. There is no exit. Or rather, there is one exit, through which all must pass. But is that the last word?

[3] For the comments on this idea which follow, see Derek Kidner, *Proverbs* (*Tyndale Old Testament Commentaries*, Inter-Varsity Press, 1964), pp. 40 f.

[4] *Ibid.*, p. 41.

[5] More literally, 'and (those who go) after them, (who) accept their mouth'; 'mouth' often refers to 'speech' (especially commands). *Cf.* BDB, p. 805a, comparing with Ec. 10:13; Is. 29:13.

A RADICAL ALTERNATIVE

Death is a human inevitability. But it threatens to make nonsense not only of the world's ways of living with life, but also of the Bible's. The biblical world-view sees God as working out a righteous purpose in the world. It believes that justice and not arbitrariness has the last word. But the belief that crime pays, or even that, at best, the fates of the wicked and the righteous are indistinguishable, because God gets the wicked too in the end (which is all that the psalmist has so far established), makes nonsense of this world-view. What else has the psalmist to offer by way of approach to the question?

A personal conviction

The psalmist has wrestled with this problem, and come to certain conclusions. That way of putting the matter, however, is misleading, for he expresses his conviction as a personal testimony. Although he belongs to the Wisdom movement, his solution is not one reached merely by thinking. It comes by revelation: *I bend my ear to instruction* given by God[6] (4a). Like a prophet, he listens for 'what the God Yahweh will say' (Ps. 85:8) to his people in need, which he can then pass on to them. Thus *I will resolve my problem in my music* (4b). He is not just a philosopher, but a psalmist, and he seeks to let a song within him (given by the Spirit, we would say) find expression—a song which will embody a solution to the enigma that has been perplexing him.

Believing that the message he will bring is given to him by God, he is confident of its truth:

> *My mouth will speak true wisdom,*
> *My heart will express its insight*[7] *(3).*

It thus demands the attention of all men, irrespective of nation or position (1–2). On the one hand, his words do not apply only to Israel. Yahweh is the God of the whole world, and the psalmist's problem is one that belongs to man as man. It is not just the religious man's question, though the answer lies only in a re-

---

[6] *Cf.* Anderson for this understanding of *māšāl*, a rather general word most frequently translated 'proverb'.

[7] Literally 'the expression of my heart will be insight'.

ligious perspective. It is a question men of many nations have asked: and it is characteristic of the Wisdom movement that it approaches the questions of man as man; it does not speak only to the covenant people.

On the other hand, the psalmist's words have implications within a nation both for *rich and poor alike* (2).[8] As we have seen, the psalm goes on to show that the former have less security than they think; the latter, if they turn to God and put their confidence in him, have more.

A divine intervention

But God . . . (15). The phrase sums up much of the message of the Bible. 'You meant it for evil, *but God* meant it for good' (Gn. 50:20); they crucified Jesus, *'but God* raised him from the dead' (Acts 13:30); we were dead through sin, *'but God,* who is rich in mercy, . . . made us alive together with Christ' (Eph. 2:4–5). Human dead ends are overcome by divine power.

The content of the psalmist's message is that the inevitable fate of the mighty and the rich, the wise and the devil-may-care, is not inevitable after all for those who look to God: for he himself *will ransom my life* (15a). The psalmist picks up expressions he has used earlier (7–8). There he has declared that paying the ransom price is humanly impossible. The 'but God', however, opens up a whole new range of possibilities. *He will surely take me from the power of Sheol* (15b): its authority is not, as the previous verse might have implied, impossible to controvert. But it does take God to storm its gates.

But what exactly does the psalmist mean? Being delivered from the power of Sheol is spoken of elsewhere (*e.g.* Pss. 18:4–5, 16–17; 86:13), where the context shows that the reference is to rescue from the danger of death—for instance, in battle or through illness. In such situations Death reaches into this world and even in this life begins to affect a man: he loses his vitality. He is not merely in danger of death; he begins to experience it.[9]

---

[8] But there is no evidence that the expressions used in verse 2a indicate also a desire to speak to *both low and high* (RSV); *all mankind, every living man* (NEB), a more generalizing translation, is more likely to be right.

[9] There is a parallel here in the Old Testament's understanding of Death's attempt (partially successful) to lord it over man in this life and to deprive him of fullness of life, with the New Testament's picture of this world as the

And so, when the Lord delivers him, it is a deliverance from death and from Sheol, which may already spoil his life and threaten soon to end it.

Psalm 49's conviction that God *will take me from the power of Sheol* could refer to this experience: the wicked have no protection when threatened by death before their time, but the righteous have God to turn to. And yet the psalm seems to promise something more than this common enough conviction (*cf.* the solemnity of the opening verses). And its argument centres not on the possibility of early death, but on the inevitability of eventual death (see verses 10–14, 17–20). It is this inevitability that the 'but God' has to counter.

Does the psalmist then expect to avoid experiencing death? *He will take me* might suggest so, for the same expression is used of Enoch and Elijah, who were 'translated' to heaven without experiencing death (Gn. 5:24; 2 Ki. 2:9–12); and this avoiding of death has been the aim expressed earlier—that a man should *live on for ever, not see the Pit* (9). Or does he expect to be taken from Sheol's power at death (or after), taken from Death's clutches to be with God? Perhaps we should accept that what is said here is allusive; perhaps there was an allusiveness about what was revealed to the psalmist.[1]

For it did not seem to be God's purpose even in the New Testament to tell men all that they might like to know about the afterlife. Certainly what was before tentative and developing is now universal and assured: Christ is risen as the first-fruits of the dead (1 Cor. 15:20) and is thus the guarantee of a full harvest. A doctrine of afterlife and resurrection is now theologically possible and apologetically defensible, as it was not before. But its description remains ambiguous. Before the resurrection are we conscious or unconscious? What is the relationship between being with Christ, being in heaven, being in paradise, being in Abraham's bosom, being in Sheol? The New Testament gives us no detailed map or programme for what happens after death; but by means of many pictures it suggests 'Relax, trust, it will be all right'.

---

domain of death and of man's failing to experience real (eternal) life and already being spiritually dead. *Cf.* Jn. 5:21–27; Rom. 8:1–11.

[1] *Cf.* Ps. 73:24, where similar expressions appear and similar considerations apply.

And this assurance is the most important element in the promise which the Lord gives the psalmist. As the New Testament expresses it, he will be with the Lord, which will actually be better than being here (Phil. 1:23). There he will find the light and life which death takes away (Rev. 22:1-5).

A sure and certain hope

If this is to be the future, what attitude does it make possible in the present?

The psalmist started from a position of fear (5). But now he can urge, *Do not be afraid*[2] *when a man becomes rich . . .* (16). The admitted inequalities of this life do not indicate that chance or injustice is life's last word. On the one side, wealth and honour are of impermanent value. On the other—again to anticipate the New Testament's fuller picture—the believer is promised 'an eternal weight of glory beyond all comparison' (2 Cor. 4:17). Therefore confidence replaces fear, and insight shows itself more valuable than wealth:

> *Man with prestige but without insight*[3]
> *Is one with the cattle doomed to slaughter* (20).

Man with the psalmist's insight, even without earthly success, finds a distinctively human destiny in being received by God into glory to enjoy him for ever.

[2] NEB emends and destroys the parallel.
[3] RSV, TEV (with some Hebrew MSS) assimilate to verse 12: more likely the difference is intentional.

Will God forgive?
(Psalm 51)

The choirmaster's.   A psalm.   David's.
When Nathan the prophet went to him, when he had had
intercourse with Bathsheba.

¹ *Be gracious to me, O God, in accordance with your covenant-love.*
In your great tenderness blot out my acts of rebellion.
² *Wash me quite clean of my waywardness,*
Cleanse me from my failings.
³ *I do recognize my acts of rebellion,*
My failings confront me constantly.
⁴ *I have failed you, you alone,*
I have done what you regard as wrong.
So you should be acknowledged as right in your sentence
And justified in giving judgment.

⁵ *Yes, I have been wayward from birth,*
I have failed you since the day of my conception.
⁶ *Yes, it is inner trustworthiness that pleases you;*
You teach me inward wisdom.

⁷ *Remove my sin with hyssop so that I can be clean.*
Wash me so that I am whiter than snow.
⁸ *Let me hear joy and gladness,*
Let the one you have broken rejoice.
⁹ *Turn your face away from my failures,*
Blot out all my wayward acts.

10 *Create me a clean mind, O God,*
   Renew in me a steadfast spirit.
11 *Do not dismiss me from your presence,*
   Do not take from me your holy spirit.
12 *Restore to me the joy of being saved by you,*
   Sustain me with your willing spirit.

13 *I will teach your ways to rebels,*
   And sinners will return to you.
14 *Deliver me from death, God my saviour.*
   I will declare the praise of your righteousness.
15 *Lord, open my lips:*
   My mouth will proclaim your praise!

16 *You would have no pleasure in sacrifice, were I to bring one.*
   You would not want a whole offering.
17 *A godly sacrifice is a broken spirit;*
   A heart that is broken and crushed you would not disdain, O God.

18 *In your graciousness deal kindly with Zion,*
   Build the walls of Jerusalem.
19 *Then find pleasure in right sacrifices,*
   In whole offerings, given over totally to you.
   Then let bulls ascend upon your altar.

'Teach mee how to repent: for that's as good
As if thou'hadst seal'd my pardon, with thy blood' (John Donne).[1]

He has sealed our pardon with his blood. But God's willingness to forgive does not heal the relationship between us and him until we respond. Without that response, God's grace achieves nothing.

There are two words that are often translated as 'repent', the act of response to the holy but gracious God. One suggests being sorry about something: about someone else's action or misfortune (*e.g.* Jdg. 2:18; 21:6, 15), or about one's own actions

---

[1] 'At the round earth's imagin'd corners, blow', lines 13-14.

(*e.g.* Je. 8:6).[2] It is a verb that indicates one's feelings of sorrow. But this sorrow is one that leads to action, as the passages referred to show. It leads to practical efforts to meet the needs of those for whom one is sorry. 'To comfort' (another form of the same word) is not just 'to console' but 'to restore' (*cf.* Is. 40:1; 49:13; 51:3, 12, 19). Similarly, it leads to practical efforts to change courses of action that one is sorry for: 'repentance' is not only a change of heart, but a change of direction.

This latter point is made explicitly by the other main Hebrew word for 'repentance', which is the regular word for turning away or turning round. Repentance means turning away from one course of action and embarking on a different one, turning from one 'way' and taking another, turning your life around (*cf.* Ps. 51:13).

Psalm 51 illustrates both the attitude of sorrow and the determination to begin a new life which are involved in repentance. Its sections and themes further unfold the elements of this turning to God.

Repentance faces up to sins (verses 1–4)

The psalm formally begins with a plea for God's grace and forgiveness (1–2). But behind that plea lies an acknowledgement of the facts of the situation between man and God. The psalmist can ask for his sins to be forgiven because he is aware of them, he is not hiding from them.

> *I do[3] recognize my acts of rebellion,*
> *My failings confront me constantly* (3).

[2] There is a series of references to God's repentance which use this word: *e.g.* Gn. 6:6–7; 1 Sa. 15:11, 35; Jon. 3:9–10; 4:2. The element of paradox in the idea of God repenting is underlined by the presence elsewhere of the contrary assertion that God does not repent (Nu. 23:19; 1 Sa. 15:29—the latter in the context of one of the references to his repentance referred to above). What is asserted by the statement that God repents is that there is a real relationship between man and God, in which man has scope for making real decisions, for making history, in God's world. God's own will is worked out in a dialectic with human decisions. And thus God changes his plans, as it were, as men exercise their initiatives. In this sense he repents (*cf.* Je. 18:8, 10). But of course he is not fickle or changeable; he can be relied on, he is wholly consistent. In this sense he does not repent.

[3] The pronoun 'I' is expressed; in Hebrew, as in other ancient languages, it does not have to be expressed, and is therefore probably emphatic here.

Later the psalmist will plead for the Lord to hide his face from his sins (9). Human beings themselves find this difficult as regards the offences of others. It is only too easy to hide from our own sins, however. Psychology has identified and labelled the phenomenon of projection, whereby we sometimes note with disapproval in others the weaknesses that we cannot face up to in ourselves. I recall regretting the 'brusqueness' of a vicar we know, and being amazed as well as hurt when my wife not only responded 'But *you* are like that', but was also able to illustrate her assertion from something which had just happened.

It was for me a moment of revelation. Before, I had not recognized that fault. From then on, it confronted me constantly! Such experiences are painful, but they are one means of growth, one way in which God leads us to seek forgiveness and renewal.

A little while ago I read Keith Miller's book *The Becomers*.[4] The title suggests an approach to the Christian life: we are seeking to become what God sees we could be. But this means facing up to specific inadequacies in what we are. It means, for instance, learning to recognize one's idolatries, those (perhaps good) things that have become more important than God. Miller suggests asking oneself what one thinks about when there is nothing else to occupy one's mind, or what sections of the newspaper one turns to first. Such instinctive interests may be one's idolatries.

As I read the book, I suspected it had something to say to me, but I could not quite crystallize it. I could not identify an idol. It is the Old Testament that I find myself thinking about when I have nothing else to do. Eventually 'the penny dropped': the Old Testament was my idol. Trying to understand it, to preach it, to write about it, absorbs and fascinates me. It was more important to me than God.

But I had resisted this insight. When the moment of realization came, everything fell into place. I had disregarded Miller's observation about the newspapers because I prefer to get down to study rather than reading them. Now I saw the significance of that. Now I saw why I found it more difficult to pray in my study than I did in the college chapel: my study was the idol's shrine.

It is with some embarrassment that I mention all this, for fear it sounds stupid; few will worship my idol, most will regard my religion as very peculiar. But others will have their own idols.

[4] Hodder and Stoughton, 1973.

And the gaining of insight into one's sins is of key importance to us if we wish to lay hold on God's forgiveness and renewing grace.

The story of David and Bathsheba, to which the heading of the psalm refers,[5] illustrates this phenomenon of repression and projection. As David proceeds from lust to adultery, from deceit to murder (2 Sa. 11), what went on in his mind? 'Why not have another woman—you have several concubines already. She's only the wife of a foreigner.' 'Better try to pass off the paternity as Uriah's—better not have a scandal.' 'If he will not co-operate, he has brought trouble on himself. A scandal would not be in the national interest.' The human mind has an amazing ability for conning itself. This is why God's laws which forbid such acts as coveting someone's wife, committing adultery and murder are such a blessing. They preserve us from having to make up our own mind from scratch as to 'what love requires' in every situation. When confronted by the naked Bathsheba, clear ground-rules are very helpful.

But despite these, David falls into several traps; and with David, as with us, it takes an indirect approach to undermine his defences against self-understanding. 'What would you think of a rich man who robbed a poor man of all he had?' 'He deserves to die!' 'The rich man is you' (2 Sa. 12:1–7). It takes a parable to get through the defences of the man who would be able to resist a frontal attack. It is for such a man, whose defences against self-understanding have been breached, that the psalm speaks.

The wayward, rebellious failure

When the veil, which formerly obscured the mirror as we looked into it, has been rent, what do we see?

The psalmist speaks of his waywardness, his rebelliousness and

[5] The usual view has been that this heading indicates the occasion on which David composed the psalm. The headings to other psalms generally seem to be liturgical rather than historical notes, however. This has led to the suggestion that the heading here indicates rather that Psalm 51 was used when this story from David's life was read in worship (so Dalglish, pp. 233–248), or that the heading aims to help people to apply the psalm to their own spiritual lives by pointing to this story as illustrating the kind of situation in which a man might use the psalm (cf. B. S. Childs, 'Psalm Titles and Midrashic Exegesis', in *Journal of Semitic Studies* 16, 1971, pp. 137–150). But see Kidner for a defence of the traditional view. The heading is omitted by NEB and put in the margin by TEV, but there is no doubt as to its place in the Hebrew text.

his failure. It is regrettable that in English words such as sin and righteousness, iniquity and salvation, transgression and repentance, are almost exclusively 'religious' words. They are not used in 'secular' contexts, like other theological words such as father and brother, guilt and reconciliation. Here, when the psalmist acknowledges his sin, he does so in words that would be familiar from everyday life.

His sin has the character of *rebellion* (1b, 3a, 13a). The Hebrew word suggests not so much transgression (as it is often translated) against a written code, as defiance in the face of lawful authority. It is the word used for the rebellion of children against their parents and for subjects' throwing off their masters' yoke, failing to keep the obligations that were laid upon them (*e.g.* 1 Ki. 12:19). Applied to the relationship between God and his people it suggests that we ought to go God's way, but do not: we refuse and defy him. 'I raised sons, I brought them up—and they rebelled against me' (Is. 1:2). Israel's rebellion consisted, to put it another way, in her failing to abide by her covenant commitment. But behind this rebellion lay man's original declaration of independence soon after his creation (Gn. 3). It was to bring rebels back to their Lord that Jesus died; but the rebellion goes on this side of the cross, as the people of God continue to ignore where the word and the Spirit direct.

His sin has the character of *waywardness* (2a, 5a, 9b).[6] The word suggests the deliberate choice of the wrong road and thus brings out something of the strange perversity of sin: does anyone deliberately choose the wrong road? Experience confirms that we do, though rationalizing the decisions as David did. Israel again offers us a mirror-image of ourselves: 'they have chosen the wrong road, they have forgotten Yahweh their God' (Je. 3:21).

His sin has the character of *failure*. The word is the most frequent one here (2b, 3b, 4a, 5b, 9a, 13b) as elsewhere in the Old Testament. Perhaps 'failure' is then the dominant note in the Old Testament's understanding of sin; and this is striking, for failure is the secularized version of sin which modern man (Christian or not) especially fears. He longs to succeed, to do well and find recognition, and the longing can be creative, a stimulus to achievement. But barely under the surface it holds the deep fear of failure which we find it hard to acknowledge. Are not this suc-

[6] EVV 'iniquity' or 'guilt'.

cess for which we yearn, this failure which we dread, the 'unknown gods' which the Old Testament identifies? 'To succeed' is to realize God's ideal. 'To fail' is to fall short of his glory (*cf.* Rom. 3:23[7]). Thus our failure is not just an experiential or psychological matter, but a moral one. For the glory of Yahweh is his holiness, and it is his holiness we fall short of.

Whom do we fail? Secular man may be aware only of failing himself, and indeed God does want us to live a full life and realize our potential. The man of a more tender conscience is aware of failing others: his parents, his children, his teachers, his pupils, his friends, his wife. And indeed the affects of sin on other people are not to be treated lightly. But these failures are also sins against God. Thus David, who had failed Bathsheba, and Uriah, and Joab, and the nameless child, acknowledges 'I have failed Yahweh' (2 Sa. 12:13); and Joseph, pursued by Potiphar's wife, asks, 'How could I do something as evil as this, and fail (not Potiphar, but) God?' (Gn. 39:9). Our moral failures with regard to other people are failures with regard to God, too. The psalmist, however, speaks of a failure that is *only* against God (4). Perhaps this is the sin that affects no human being, the sin that no-one sees.[8] Perhaps, like Paul (Phil. 3:4–6), Job (Jb. 31), and many other psalmists (*e.g.* Ps. 44:17–18), he could claim to be relatively sinless, successful in his outward morality, committed to keeping the commandments. If so, the relative goodness of his outward life (not something to be despised) throws into relief the darkness within him. Perhaps, again, the sinner that speaks is the nation in exile (as it certainly is in verses 18–19), aware of the sins that it had committed against Yahweh alone: the sins of failure to trust in God, of worshipping other gods, for which the prophets have indicted the nation and which have finally brought its downfall. The story of the people of God is a story of rebellion, waywardness and failure.

The justification of God (verse 4)

Facing up to the facts about sin thus involves looking them in the eye oneself. But it also means doing this before God, acknowledging the appropriateness of his assessment of oneself. It means

---

[7] The standard Greek word for 'sin', *hamartanō*, which appears here, also means 'to fail' or 'to miss the mark'; and *cf.* Jdg. 20:16.

[8] So Gunkel, in his comment on the passage.

coming to see them as he sees them, and recognizing that his attitude is right.

> *I have failed you, you alone,*
> *I have done what you regard as wrong.*
> *So you should be acknowledged as right in your sentence*
> *And justified in giving judgment.*

Getting things off one's chest can be a therapeutic exercise. One may feel better afterwards, when one is no longer bottling things up, when the skeletons are out of the cupboard. On the other hand, of course, the process may lead only to a feeling of helplessness and depression. The past is irretrievable; it cannot be undone. Even when expressed openly, its haunting power may not be exorcized.

The psalmist is not seeking therapy, however. It is not a question of acknowledging my sins so that I will feel better, but of acknowledging my sins so that you will be seen to be justified.[9] Nor is the psalmist expressing despair, as if it were a question of acknowledging my sins, but feeling that there is nothing to be achieved by doing so. Rather the psalmist is acknowledging his sin, and thereby taking his place again within the meaningful context of the will of God. He realizes that he has no claim upon God. But he believes that fulfilling the function that he can within the will of God at this point (that is, testifying openly to his justice) is the only place where there *may* be hope, where he *may* be able to find a new start.

Such a new start cannot be presumed upon. It was not granted

[9] Verse 4 more literally says 'I have failed you . . . *so that you may* be acknowledged as right . . .' (*cf.* NEB). The 'so that' should not be watered down into 'with the result that' (*cf.* BDB, p. 775b), as it is in RSV. The literal translation suggests the striking thought that sin fulfils an intended purpose (not, of course, intended by the sinner) of contributing to the glory of God, perhaps by providing the dark background which throws his holiness and justice into sharper light. Paul alludes to this verse in Rom. 3:4, and (since he goes on to speak explicitly of our wickedness showing God's justice) commentators generally assume that this is the point he is making in this verse. But the idea of Ps. 51:4 probably is that my confession glorifies God (rather than that my sin glorifies God); Anderson's suggestion that there is an ellipse of a phrase such as 'I confess that' at the beginning of verse 4 seems the most likely understanding of the verse.

to Achan, who responded to Joshua's exhortation to 'give glory to Yahweh the God of Israel, and acknowledge him' by confessing the secret sin he had committed which had brought judgment on the people (Jos. 7:19). Despite his confession, he had to accept punishment; yet the story suggests that he died with honour and meaning in that he had 'justified God' at the end of his life.

So the psalmist speaks as a man who is 'down', *broken* (8). Why is that? Has God been unfair to him? No. He acknowledges his sin in order to acknowledge that his suffering is deserved. He may have been moral in public, but he has been a sinner in private, and so has deserved what he experiences. Or, if we hear the psalm on the lips of God's people in exile, we hear their acknowledgement that the exile does not evidence the capriciousness or the feebleness of Israel's God, but rather his justice. The psalm is, in fact, like the books of Kings with their reign-by-reign acknowledgement of Israel's sin which makes judgment God's entirely appropriate response. The books are 'an act of praise at the justice of the judgement of God'.[1] It is a confession that contributes to the justification of God.

Repentance recognizes sin (verses 5–6)

The following verses move on from the fact of sins to the depth of sin. How long has the psalmist been wayward? Since he was a rebellious teenager? How long has failure haunted him? Since the 11-plus? The demon failure has haunted him since he was born: it is the very atmosphere he breathed from the first (5).

The commentators hasten to assert, when they come to this verse, that the psalm is not here teaching the doctrine of original sin.[2] If they mean that he is not suggesting that there is some-

---

[1] A long English paraphrase of the one German word *Gerichtsdoxologie*, used by von Rad (I, pp. 342 f., 357 f.) in his discussion of Kings, Ps. 51, and the case of Achan; the English rendering comes, however, from P. R. Ackroyd, *Exile and Restoration* (*Old Testament Library*, SCM Press, 1968), p. 78. Kraus, too, picks up the expression in his comment on Ps. 51:4, and compares also Luther's reference to the 'justification of God'. *Cf.* also Paul's argument in Rom. 3:19–26.

[2] 'Original Sin standeth not in the following of *Adam*, (as the *Pelagians* do vainly talk;) but it is the fault and corruption of the Nature of every man, that naturally is ingendered of the offspring of *Adam*; whereby man is very far

thing sinful about the act through which a child is conceived, or that sin is genetically transmitted (as that doctrine has sometimes been thought to imply), then the point may be granted.[3] But if the doctrine of original sin asserts that there is something fundamentally askew about human existence, that it is affected by sin through and through, then the psalm's way of thinking does not seem so different. Human beings are not like the curate's egg; the bad smell pervades the whole. Even my best deeds are affected by my mixed motives.

This is true of the individual. It is also true of the people of God as a whole. Israel often pictured herself as one person, as a 'corporate personality'. Extending the metaphor, she could see her history as the story of one man. And the idea of sinfulness going back to the very beginning of her life applied here too (Ezk. 16); hence her need of a new heart (Ezk. 36:26), of the renewal of the very centre of her personality. It is thus possible to hear this psalm on the lips of God's people under chastisement for their sin. The church, too, is sinful through and through, and always in need of reformation. The purity of the church will be achieved only in heaven.

So the psalmist moves on from 'I have sinned (and confess it), so that you may be shown to be right', to 'Yes, I recognize the depth of my sin. Yes, you have been opening my eyes to the truth'.[4]

> *Yes, I have been wayward from birth,*
> *I have failed you since the day of my conception.*

---

gone from original righteousness, and is of his own nature inclined to evil . . .' (The Church of England *Articles of Religion*, IX).

[3] Though the Bible comes close to speaking in such terms elsewhere. One of the few things that Job, Eliphaz and Bildad agree on is that clean cannot be born from unclean (Jb. 14:4; 15:14; 25:4; *cf.* Jn. 3:6); compare the laws regarding uncleanness (Lv. 12). We might prefer to express the point in environmental terms—a child is born into and brought up in an environment that is characterized by sin, and it is inevitable that he is affected by this, as by other aspects of his environment. The point is still that a man's oneness with the human race is a oneness in sin.

[4] In verses 4–6 there is a double movement from man to God, which these two summary phrases seek to give expression to. The two halves of verse 4 are connected by 'so that'; verses 5 and 6 are connected by the 'yes' (*hēn*) with which they both begin. EVV mostly obscure the structure here by their translation, or by their paragraphing.

Yes, it is inner trustworthiness that pleases you; [5]
You teach me inward wisdom [6] (5-6).

The two verses highlight the contrast between the waywardness and failure which characterize men, and the trustworthiness and insight which are God's concerns. The psalmist has become aware of this contrast, aware not only of having committed offences that cannot be overlooked, but also of having carried on a life that cannot be corrected. He is aware of this because God has granted him the insight. God has broken through those barriers to self-knowledge to which we referred, and led him into the beginnings of an understanding of the truth—the truth about himself. He has seen the radicalness of God's interests in a man, and he is beginning to accept them.

Repentance appeals to God's love (verse 1)

The psalmist stands in court, and pleads guilty. Why should he be let off? There is no claim to diminished responsibility. On what basis, then, can he ask for acquittal?

He begins with an appeal to God's grace, to God's covenant-loyalty, and to God's feelings. These are the first phrases that come in the psalm, before there is any reference to his sin. It was the latter, however, that constituted his hidden agenda, even from the beginning, so we have looked at that first. Indeed we are now in a position to appreciate how much is to be asked of the grace, the covenant-loyalty and the feelings of God.

The psalmist is fortunate in having grounds for believing that these aspects of God will bear the weight he has to place upon them, for the words go back to near the beginning of Israel's life with God. After her redemption from Egypt, and while she awaits Moses' descent from Mount Sinai, she soon falls into devising her own idolatrous way of worship and thus manifests the rebelliousness that will characterize her whole story. She deserves to be cast off. But she is not! And there at Sinai a new

[5] More literally, 'you approve of trustworthiness in the covered parts'. NEB's alternative interpretation connects the verb with a root known otherwise only from Arabic. Note that *truth* (*'emet*) characteristically denotes in Hebrew not mere factual accuracy, but personal reliability.

[6] Some EVV take this line as the beginning of the psalmist's prayer, but this understanding seems to underestimate the significance of the indications of structure referred to in note 4 above.

revelation of God is given. He manifests himself in these circumstances as 'Yahweh, Yahweh, the God tender[7] and gracious,[8] slow to anger but rich in covenant-loyalty[9] and trustworthiness,[1] one who shows his loyalty to thousands, who forgives waywardness, rebellion and failure'[2] (Ex. 34:6–7; *cf.* 33:19). That forgiving grace will be needed again and again if God's people are not to be destroyed at a stroke. Thus it is often alluded to in these terms in the Old Testament.[3] And it is its promise which the psalmist appeals to here: *Be gracious to me, O God, in accordance with your covenant-love. In your great tenderness.* . . .

He refers first to God's *grace*,[4] which means in the Old Testament, as it does in the New, the favourable attitude shown though not earned. Like other theological words we have considered, it is at home as much in everyday secular life as in theology: as we speak of doing someone a favour (a deed we were not obliged to perform), so Ruth speaks of finding favour with someone who will let her glean in his field (Ru. 2:2). Grace or favour is the unearned, positive, friendly, giving attitude of someone. As a sinner, the psalmist appeals to his knowledge that God, though he cannot be presumed on, is by nature gracious. The sinner can come to him only with empty, indeed dirty, hands, 'Just as I am, without one plea'; but God's own character of graciousness means that the sinner nevertheless comes in hope of the acceptance that he has indeed not earned.

He appeals secondly to the *love* and the *loyalty* that God shows as he keeps the commitment he makes within the covenant. English lacks even a near-equivalent to this word.[5] 'Steadfast love' (RSV), 'goodness' (JB), 'true love' (NEB), 'kindness' (Gelineau), 'constant love' (TEV), all express aspects of the idea, though perhaps none conveys the important note of keeping a commitment, which the word suggests. The word belongs to a reciprocal

---

[7] The root which appears in Ps. 51:1b.

[8] The root which appears at the beginning of verse 1.

[9] The word which appears at the end of 1a.

[1] The word which appears in 6a.

[2] The three words for sin which appear frequently in the psalm.

[3] *Cf.* Nu. 14:18; Ne. 9:17; Pss. 86:15; 103:8; 111:4; 112:4; 116:5; 145:8; Joel 2:13; Jon. 4:2; Na. 1:3; 2 Ch. 30:9 (B. S. Childs, *Exodus*, Old Testament Library, SCM Press, 1974, p. 619).

[4] Most EVV translate the verb here as 'be merciful', but this is misleading.

[5] *ḥeseḏ.* See also the comment on 43:1, above, p. 32.

relationship which two parties have promised to keep. The implication of the word is that the psalmist does in fact reckon that he has a claim on God! The point must not be put too unequivocally, for 'covenant-loyalty' is a two-sided affair, and the psalmist acknowledges that he has not kept his side of the commitment. In this sense, he cannot complain if God stops keeping his side. And yet, the commitment has revealed something of the purpose of God, and the instinct of the repentant sinner is surely right when he appeals to the commitment that God himself has entered into; for the gifts and the call of God are irrevocable (Rom. 11:29). All the more boldly may God's people appeal to his covenant-loyalty when they do not seem to be in a state of sin (*cf.* Ps. 44:23–26, which closes with an appeal to this covenant-love).

The psalmist refers, thirdly, to God's *tenderness* (JB), his 'mercy' (RSV) or 'compassion' (Gelineau): he appeals to God's feelings. The word is connected with the one for 'womb', and apparently refers to the kind of feelings that brothers (from the same womb) have for each other, or that a mother has for the children of her womb (*cf.* Is. 49:15). So, as well as recalling God's inner nature as grace, and the commitment of his will to the covenant, the psalmist alludes to the pull of God's feelings towards his people. God is his Lord, whose favour he may seek; his ally, whose loyalty he may expect; his brother, whose sympathy he may depend on.

Repentance pleads for forgiveness (verses 1–2, 7–9)

On the basis of the appeal to God's love which we have just examined, the psalmist goes on actually to seek forgiveness; first fairly summarily (1b–2), then, after his developed acknowledgement of sin (3–6), at greater length (7–9). He uses a variety of pictures to describe the forgiveness he seeks; the ones in 1b–2 recur in 7–9, so we will look at the former as we work through the latter.

Forgiveness is like the removing of defilement (7a, 2b). As we have noted, some biblical ideas are easier for us to appreciate than others, because they are still in common use in our world. Others depend on religious practices and attitudes that we are mostly less familiar with, and the idea of uncleanness is one of these. It is difficult to define, but easy enough to illustrate: many animals are unclean (Lv. 11; Dt. 14); childbirth and a wide range of emissions and skin conditions make one unclean (Lv. 12–15); anything connected with death makes one unclean (Nu. 19:11–16). The basis for these categorizations is probably sometimes hygienic, sometimes religious (some animals forbidden were sacred to other gods); but underlying it is also a more basic feeling of instinctive revulsion, such as many today would have in the presence of a dead body. Thus someone who is unclean is tainted and to be avoided. He cannot take part in worship or in social life. He is an outcast. The leper with his bell warning others of his presence is the epitome of this phenomenon.

Many instances of uncleanness can be dealt with by ritual purification. For instance, the cleansed 'leper'[6] is restored after a rite involving the sprinkling of blood with hyssop (Lv. 14:1–7). The uncleanness that results from contact with the dead is removed after a rite involving the sprinkling of water with hyssop (Nu. 19:14–19).

Clearly the notion of ritual defilement reflected in such passages as these is applied in the psalm as a picture of the moral state of man before God; he asks for a cleansing that is analogous to the sprinkling rites prescribed by the law. Like a man defiled, he pictures himself as a social outcast, repugnant to other men, to God and to himself, and pleads, *Remove my sin with hyssop*[7] *so that I can be clean*. To make someone clean with regard to some physical cause of uncleanness may require a miracle (*cf.* the stories of Naaman, 2 Ki. 5, and of the ten lepers, Lk. 17:11–19); how much more the moral cleansing for which the psalmist asks.

Forgiveness is like washing nappies (7b, 2a). Verse 7 continues with a picture that is similar, but significantly different: it speaks of the kind of dirt that you can see only too clearly. *Wash me so that I am whiter than snow*: the expression is not one used for washing oneself, but one that refers to the washing of clothes by treading them. It suggests not a polite rinse but a thorough[8] scrub, which

[6] References to leprosy perhaps deserve to be put in inverted commas, as the equivalent Hebrew word covers a much wider range of complaints than the disease called leprosy in English.

[7] A bushy plant used for sprinkling.

[8] The point is made explicit by the 'thoroughly' (*quite*) of 2a; the thoroughness of cleansing corresponds to the 'thoroughness' of mercy (*your great tenderness*) in the previous half-line: the word we have translated 'great' comes from the same root.

presupposes that the object of washing is in a thoroughly dishevelled state.

> 'Though you scrub yourselves with soap
> And use quantities of detergent,
> Your waywardness stains you in my sight' (Je. 2:22).

This is how the psalmist feels. He is doing his best to do his part, to scrub his heart clean from evil (*cf.* Je. 4:14). But he knows that the real cleaning up work has to be done by God himself. Only he can wash whiter than white the garments that are a spectacular and unmistakably vivid red (*cf.* Is. 1:18).[9] All the soap powder commercials we have ever seen may help to bring the psalmist's point home for us.

Forgiveness is like hearing someone say, 'That's all right' (verse 8). Fairly often I have to say 'sorry' to my wife, usually over fairly small things. As I open the front door, my heart sinks as I realize I am still holding the letter she asked me to make sure I posted. 'Love, I'm sorry, I forgot to post that letter.' It is a moment of suspense as I wait to find out whether the response will be silence or 'It's OK, I can always take it myself later on'. Sometimes husbands and wives have to confess much worse lapses, and the suspense and anxiety must be much more profound. 'How will she react?' 'What will he say?'

So it is when a man comes to God. The psalmist longs to *hear* words that will bring *joy and gladness* back to him. The Old Testament includes various examples of prayers for restoration, for help, for guidance, receiving clear answers from a prophet or some other mouthpiece of God (*e.g.* Is. 37:15–35; 2 Ch. 20:1–17; Pss. 12; 60; 85). The other great psalm of penitence, Psalm 130, looks for Yahweh's word of response in a similar way to Psalm 51. Both long for Yahweh to say, through his priest or prophet, 'It's all right'; 'Your sins are forgiven'; or, as Nathan actually said to David, 'Yahweh has removed your sin. You will not die' (2 Sa. 12:13). As Luther comments, 'When you become sad or feel divine wrath, do not look for any other medicine or accept

---

[9] The opposite of white in Scripture is red; one of our black students reminds me that sin is not described as black in the Bible, and that our black brothers would appreciate it if we did not so describe it either. I do not know where this leaves us in relation to the American Indians, however!

any other solace than the Word, whether it is spoken by a brother who is present or comes from the spirit remembering a word you had heard earlier . . . In the use of the Sacraments and in confession we teach men to look mainly at the Word.'[1]

Hearing Yahweh's word of forgiveness will mean his transition from brokenness to joy:

> *Let me hear* (words of) *joy and gladness.*
> *Let the one*[2] *you have broken rejoice.*

The psalmist is a broken man, crushed by the weight of his sin, and that of God's own doing. But the God who broke him is also the one who can heal him, restore him, make the man who was broken into a man who is rejoicing.[3]

Forgiveness is like wiping the slate clean (9b, 1b). Neither our names nor our lives, neither who we are nor what we have done, escapes God's attention and memory. One way the Bible makes this point is by speaking of a heavenly record book which details them. Sometimes this is referred to as a list of the names of the people of God, a heavenly *Who's Who* to which we all belong. It is the book God has written (Ex. 32:32), the book of the living or the roll of the righteous (Ps. 69:28)[4]; a good book to be in.

But God evidently also keeps a record of deeds, to be opened at the judgment (Dn. 7:10). It contains an account of good deeds (Ne. 13:14; Mal. 3:16), and of our sufferings (Ps. 56:8): but the

[1] From Luther's comments on the passage.

[2] More literally 'the bones'. As we have noted with other words, such as those for 'soul' and 'heart', Hebrew uses words for parts of man to refer to man as a whole looked at from a certain viewpoint; and, like English expressions such as '(having) nerves' or '(getting it off one's) chest' or '(having a big) heart', they are not to be interpreted too anatomically. So also the health or ill-health of the 'bones' refers at least as much to one's psychological as to one's physical well-being (*cf.* Pss. 6:2; 31:10; 35:10; Is. 38:13; 58:11; 66:14).

[3] 'Joy and gladness' is almost a stock phrase, especially in Isaiah and Jeremiah, in connection both with the threat as to what will be lost when Yahweh punishes sin, and with the promise as to what will be restored when people repent. In the time of sin, joy and gladness are inappropriate (Is. 22:12-13) and will be taken away (Je. 7:34; 16:9; 25:10); the man of God in this situation finds joy and gladness only in Yahweh's word (Je. 15:16). But they will again replace sorrow and sighing when Yahweh's ransomed ones return to Zion (Is. 35:10; 51:11); the transforming of brokenness to joy is like the blossoming of the desert (Je. 33:10-11).

[4] *Cf.* Is. 4:3; Dn. 12:1; Rev. 3:5; 13:8.

latter are recorded because they are caused by the evil deeds of others, which God does not forget. Thus, when the psalmist calls for justice upon the wicked, he prays for God to remember what his book contains (Ps. 109:13–14). But since we are all sinners, we have to face up to the fact that his books list our misdeeds, too. Yet the same God declares, 'I myself am the one who blots out your acts of rebellion on my own account. I will not call your sins to mind' (Is. 43:25). 'On my own account': because of my own character, because I am a God of grace and loyalty and compassion (Ps. 51:1). On this basis, the psalmist comes as a penitent and pleads, *blot out all my wayward acts* (9b), *blot out my acts of rebellion* (1b). Far from treasuring the memory of them, *turn your face away from my failures* (9a). As matters stand, they are before his face, demanding his attention (Ps. 90:8); they cause him to turn his face from us (Is. 59:2). The psalmist appeals to God to turn his face rather from looking at the sins, to hurl them into the depths of the sea (Mi. 7:19), to remove them as far as east is from west (Ps. 103:12).[5]

An endorsement on one's driving licence can be removed after three years; it is thought to be no longer relevant to one's driving standard now. Sins do not run out in this way (*cf.* verse 5). But God can erase them because of what he is. He erases them so effectively from his record that he never says, on some future occasion, 'Oh, you've done that again, have you?' He cannot say that, because he has forgotten the first occasion.[6]

Repentance longs for spiritual renewal (verses 10–12)

A sign that regret about the past is genuine is the desire for change in the future. The psalmist goes on from the plea for forgiveness to the plea for re-creation; we move from a concern with justification to a concern with sanctification.

[5] The Israelites were not fond of the sea (consider the story of Jonah for their expectation of what happened to the seafarer!), and the first of these two images is thus a more powerful one for them than it may be for us. Until the last decade or two, one might have regarded 'into space' as an equivalent; perhaps, indeed, despite space travel, our increasing idea of the vast dimensions of the cosmos may still make this a forceful image. As for the second image, perhaps this is rendered more forceful by the awareness that the distance from east to west is infinity!

[6] When I heard this illustration, it was attributed to Dr Kenneth Moynagh. The anthropomorphism is overstated, of course, but it makes the point vividly.

There is a move involved, and yet these two may be seen as two sides of the same coin. It is striking in our psalm that the same terms that have appeared in the plea for forgiveness reappear in the prayer for renewed spirituality. The psalmist re-expresses his concern with cleanness (10a; *cf.* 7a), with the turning away of God's face (11a; *cf.* 9a), and with the restoration of joy (12a; *cf.* 8a). The theological truth that lies behind these points of connection is the fact that forgiveness actually is the great motive power behind sanctification. It is because I have died to sin (that is, paid its penalty, in that Christ has died for me and made it possible for me to be forgiven) that sin no longer has any power over me (*cf.* Rom. 6:1–14). Dealing with the past makes it possible to begin a new future.

That is not the whole story, however. To put it in Christian terms, Calvary is followed by Pentecost; Christ dies for us, but then gives us his Spirit. Strikingly, in Psalm 51 the new plea which the prayer for renewal brings is concerned with the activity of the spirit (10b, 11b, 12b).

The spirit, in Old Testament as in New, speaks of the unseen but very real presence and power of God. The fact that the same word, both in Hebrew and in Greek, refers also to breath and to wind helps to make this point. The spirit suggests the breath, whose presence indicates the presence of life itself. The spirit suggests the power of the wind, invisible and unpredictable (*cf.* Jn. 3:8).[7]

In the Old Testament, the spirit does not come upon the members of God's people individually. The endowment of the spirit is given to such figures as kings and prophets, whom God himself especially endows for his service; it is through this endowment given to Israel's leaders that the spirit affects the nation as a whole (*e.g.* Is. 63:7–14). In Old Testament times, the hope of a promiscuous outpouring of the spirit remained a hope (Joel 2:28–29); but the fulfilling of that promise after the death and resurrection of Christ makes it possible for each Christian to pray the psalmist's prayer for the renewing of the spirit.[8] But what exactly is the psalmist seeking?

[7] See further Gn. 1:2 (where, in fact, NEB translates 'wind'); Ex. 15:8, 10; Is. 31:3; and especially Ezk. 37:1–14 (where Ezekiel makes capital of the word's threefold meaning in relating his vision).

[8] The connection of the spirit with such figures as kings and prophets supports the suggestion that this psalm is either a royal psalm or a community

First, a spiritual commitment (10). *Create me a clean mind, O God.* There is again here a recognition of the depth of the psalmist's problem with sin. He needs a new act of creation,[9] a re-creating of his very 'heart', 'the centre of human existence . . . the seat of all feeling, thinking, and willing'.[1] It is a radical remaking from within which is required, the same one promised by Ezekiel (36:25–27; *cf.* Je. 31:33). *Renew in me a steadfast[2] spirit*: one that is firm and reliable, determined and committed, prepared and set to go God's way.[3] The sinner is aware of his fickleness and unfaithfulness, and his deliverance from this must also be God's achievement.

Second, a spiritual presence (11). The spirit of God signifies the presence of God, and this point lies behind the parallelism of this verse:

> *Do not dismiss me from your presence,*
> *Do not take from me your holy spirit.*[4]

'Do not cast me from your presence; nor take your presence from me.' The picture of the previous verse was of the transcendent activity of the creator God; it was, perhaps, an 'I–it' relationship between God and the heart. Here the picture is of an immanent

---

psalm; it is less likely to be one of a single, private individual. It will be noted that we have spelt 'spirit' consistently thus without a capital letter (*cf.* most EVV). While capitalizing may be appropriate in translating the New Testament, where the doctrine of the Spirit is more systematically formulated in the light of Pentecost, in the Old Testament the spirit is only one of several ways of speaking of the presence of God (*cf.*, for instance, 'face', 'name' and 'glory'), and it would be misleading within the Old Testament's terms to give one of these expressions special treatment.

[9] The verb *bārā'* is used only of God's creative work, of what he alone can do.

[1] From Kraus's comment on the passage; see also on 44:18, above, p. 64.

[2] Oddly (in that *rûaḥ* is feminine) the adjective, or more accurately participle, *nākôn* is masculine; possibly a more literal translation would be 'the spirit of a steadfast man'.

[3] *Cf.* Pss. 57:7; 78:37; 112:7; 1 Sa. 7:3; Ezr. 7:10; Jb. 11:13.

[4] This actual phrase comes in the Old Testament only here and in Is. 63:10–11; but (if we are to take note of what it meant to the psalmist, and to refrain from reading it as if it were in the New Testament) it should not be taken as a technical phrase, but as parallel to such expressions as 'holy name'. It does draw attention, however, to the fact that the presence of the spirit is the presence of the righteous and mighty God himself.

activity, an 'I–thou' relationship. It is because there is a real two-way relationship between God and man that there is something which can be broken. It has to be kept up, to be fostered. The psalmist knows that the way he is inclined to treat God imperils the very existence of it. God could withdraw his presence, and yet that very presence is needed if he is to get anywhere near spiritual renewal.

Third, spiritual support (12). *Restore to me the joy of being saved by you*: that joy, too, is relevant to renewal, for it is a powerful stimulus to faithfulness henceforth. *Sustain me with your willing spirit*.[5] Here is a recognition that the spiritual renewal which the psalmist seeks will need to be no once-for-all event. He will be in constant need of God's sustaining, God's support. He will need God to lean on. He will be in continuous need of the resources that lie only in him.

Repentance looks forward to testimony (verses 13–15)

It is some verses since the psalmist spoke of 'I'. 'I' had been prominent in the first part of the psalm—'*I* am a sinner'. But then God became the subject of the verbs—'Will *you* forgive and renew?' Now 'I' appears again, referring not to past actions, nor to present state, but to promises for the future—'Then *I* will give you praise'.

It is the prospect of testimony and praise that dominates verses 13–15. We may well think of testimony and praise as two different exercises; one testifies to men, the other gives praise to God. The psalms, however, see them as two ways of speaking of the same activity. When God answers our prayers, we respond by telling him how great he is; but we do so in public, and this is of the essence of the matter. I was recently in a prayer meeting where we were invited to praise God silently in our hearts. As the Psalms see it, that is a nonsense. Partly this is because, if we really want to praise God, this will be something that normally demands outward expression. Enthusiasm is not embodied in silent appreciation—though there is, of course, such a thing as silent adoration.

[5] *Cf.* AV and Dahood (a rare combination) for the recognition that *God's* spirit is referred to, as in the previous verses: the expressions in 10b, 11b and 12b are so closely parallel (in each, the word for 'and the spirit' begins the half-line, being then immediately followed by its qualifying adjectival expression) that it is difficult to believe that (for instance) the first and third refer to the human spirit, the second to the divine (as RSV seems to imply).

But also praise will normally be vocal and audible because it thereby glorifies God by telling others of his deeds, so that they may be led to a deeper trust in and obedience to him. So we praise God 'in the congregation' (Ps. 107:32; *cf.* 40:7–11; 109:30; 111:1); and we praise God 'among the nations' (108:3). The Lord's deeds on his people's behalf are his way of revealing himself to the world, and the way they come to acknowledge him is through his people's praise of him.

Thus the psalms that pray for God to answer prayer often go on to promise to give God this public testimony when the prayer is answered (*cf.* 22:22–31; 69:30–33). And so it is here.

The psalmist promises to *teach* (13). He acknowledges that he is himself a rebel and a failure, but he trusts that God is going to forgive and to restore him. Then he looks forward to being able to minister to others who are like him: *I will teach your ways*[6] *to rebels, and sinners will return to you.* He will be able to explain from his own experience what are the ways of God: how he is merciful and forgiving to those who repent. And thus he will be able to win them to repentance. The person who has submitted himself to teaching, who has learnt to be a disciple, can then become a teacher (*cf.* Is. 50:4).

The psalmist promises to *testify* (14). *Deliver me from death,*[7] *God my saviour. I will declare the praise of your righteousness.* If he does not give his testimony to the righteousness and mercy of God,

---

[6] Yahweh's ways are, first, the actions characteristic of him: Ps. 138, rather similarly to 51, looks forward to praising God after he has answered the psalmist's prayer, and thus giving public testimony to Yahweh's deeds (*cf.* 138:4–7). His ways are then the acts he approves of, acts which are like his, which are taught to the nations (Is. 2:3) and are to be followed by his people (*e.g.* Pss. 119:3; 128:1). But the first fits best here. There are no passages where the expression means the way *to* Yahweh (*cf.* NEB, JB here).

[7] Literally 'from blood'; in the Bible, blood often stands for death, and normally for violent death, for the obvious reason that the presence of blood usually means the presence of death. Possibly the psalmist means 'deliver me from shedding blood' (*cf.* NEB); but there is no indication why the psalmist should pray such a prayer. Alternatively, however, the reference could be to deliverance from having my blood shed; but again, the psalm offers no other reason for suspecting that the psalmist fears either that men are about to attack him, or that he is about to be punished with death by God; though it is true that David, both for his adultery with Bathsheba and for his murder of Uriah, might see himself as in this danger. In the context of the psalm, the most likely reference is to the penalty for failing to warn someone of the mortal danger that they were in; *cf.* Ezk. 33:1–9.

and urge rebels like himself to return to God, their own blood will be on his head (Ezk. 33:8), because he will be responsible for their dying in sin. But he is determined to give that testimony. Thus, as the psalmist's chastisement reveals God's righteousness, in that he does not ignore sin (4), so salvation reveals God's righteousness, in that he does not ignore the penitent pleas of his people in their need. On what basis God can be 'both just and the justifier', however, is not actually explicit. Is not God compromising his holiness in forgiving sinners, even if they are repentant? The psalm assumes he is not; it will not be till much later that it can be seen how (cf. Rom. 3:21–26).

The psalmist promises to surrender his voice for God to use (15). At the moment his lips are sealed, because he has nothing to sing about. But if God restores him, he will thereby put a new song in his mouth (Ps. 40:2–3; cf. 30:11–12), and undo one of the saddest effects of sin. The barriers between men and God mean that they need God's grace if they are even to begin speaking with him. The point is well taken by the prayer book, which sets this verse from the psalm at the beginning of Morning and Evening Prayer. A man's legs may carry him to church, but he needs God to open his mouth with praise. This is the regular condition even of Christian men; it is especially the case for the Christian who realizes that he is spiritually 'dry'. Here is the prayer appropriate for a man like the psalmist, or for any of us at the beginning of any day:

> *Lord, open my lips:*
> *My mouth will proclaim your praise!*

Repentance offers the sacrifices God looks for (verses 16–19)

When a man asked God to deliver him, he customarily promised to return not only with words of thanksgiving, but also with a concrete expression of that in sacrifice.[8] The psalmist here alludes to the possibility of bringing a *sacrifice* or a *whole offering*, the God-ordained ways of expressing fellowship and grateful commitment. But they were only outward forms. They were thus meaningful only when the corresponding inner attitude was there; and they were ultimately dispensable. In the exile, they had to be

[8] See the comments on 50:8, above, p. 125.

dispensed with, when the temple was desolated and the priesthood taken off to Babylon, and it may be that the psalm reflects this situation (*cf.* verses 18, 19) but declares its conviction that real worship is nevertheless not impossible in the absence of sacrifice.

> *You would have no pleasure in sacrifice, were I to bring one.*[9]
> *You would not want a whole offering.*
> *A godly*[1] *sacrifice is a broken spirit;*
> *A heart that is broken and crushed you would not disdain* (16–17).

As Luther notes,[2] the psalmist speaks not of the sacrifice of praise, but of the sacrifice of humility. In the situation of wilful sin, mere sacrifice can achieve nothing. All a man can do is cast himself on God's mercy. But God is won over by those who face him with nothing.

A broken will or spirit contrasts with the hard, immalleable one to which the Old Testament often refers (*e.g.* Ps. 95:8; Is. 63:17; and classically Pharaoh, Ex. 4–14). The stubborn will has to be shattered if a man is to be led back into the ways of God, if he is to be open to God's voice. The man who has been broken can then be built up again by God himself, rebuilt in God's image.

These thoughts take us down a road which seems to lead right out of institutional religion. The temple and its worship belong to a different world; the psalm points us down the road which leads to the spiritual sacrifice offered by Christ, and to the brokenness which is the church's calling as she, too, offers her spiritual sacrifice. This being the case, the final verses of the psalm are a surprise.

> *In your graciousness*[3] *deal kindly with Zion,*
> *Build the walls of Jerusalem.*
> *Then find pleasure in right sacrifices,*

[9] Taking the last clause with the first half of the line.

[1] EVV *my sacrifice, O God* involves only the omission of one dot (*zibḥî* for *zibḥê*) and keeps the personal note of the prayer.

[2] Referred to by Kraus in his comment on the passage.

[3] The noun picks up the verb of 16b, which is from the same root; the verb from 16a similarly reappears in the last verse.

In whole offerings, given over totally to you.[4]
Then let bulls ascend[5] *upon your altar* (18–19).

If the psalm belongs to the period before the exile (if, for instance, it does go back to David), then presumably these two final verses were added in the exile to 'bring it up-to-date'.[6] They also bring it back down-to-earth. It was not God's demand that his people should live without the outward forms of temple and sacrifice. In a sense we do move a step back from the radicalism of the preceding verses, but this is because God recognizes that people need these outward forms, even if he does not.

The church seems to need them, too. Even the most anti-institutional bodies have their outward forms. Christianity has no material temple of God, and yet we have noted that Christians who pride themselves on being 'biblical' often speak of the bricks-and-mortar church as 'God's house'. Looked at from the outside, the life of the average church or Christian Union looks like just a cultic club for those who like to spend certain specified hours on Sunday and Wednesday in prescribed religious practices. God's radicalness is often too much for his people.

But fortunately he goes with them in their need of the outward and formal. He asks only that the sacrifices may be *right*: which is unlikely to mean only 'offered according to the right outward form' (though it will include that), but will also signify 'offered with the right inner attitude' of humble praise, which is the sacrifice God looks for and which is, on the human side, the condition that decides 'if God will forgive'.

---

[4] Literally 'whole offerings and whole offerings' (but two different words). The line is regarded by NEB as a later explanatory addition, but this seems no reason to omit it.

[5] 'Whole offering' is *ᶜôlāh*, from the verb 'ascend', *ᶜālāh*.

[6] So Kidner, in his comments on the passage.